CRAB

CRAB

50 RECIPES WITH THE FRESH TASTE OF THE SEA

from the Pacific, Atlantic & Gulf Coasts

CYNTHIA NIMS

Photography by Jim Henkens

SASQUATCH BOOKS
SEATTLE

Printed in China

Published by Sasquatch Books

20 19 18 17 16   9 8 7 6 5 4 3 2 1

Editor: Gary Luke
Production editor: Em Gale
Design: Joyce Hwang

Photographs (except page 7, courtesy of the author) and food styling: Jim Henkens
Copyeditor: Michael Townley

Library of Congress Cataloging-in-Publication Data is available.

ISBN: 978-1-63217-073-6

Sasquatch Books
1904 Third Avenue, Suite 710
Seattle, WA 98101
(206) 467-4300
www.sasquatchbooks.com
custserv@sasquatchbooks.com

TO BOB, WHO MEANS
THE WORLD TO ME

CONTENTS

BASICS

ICONIC CRAB

When Captain George Vancouver explored the Strait of Juan de Fuca at the north edge of Washington State's Olympic Peninsula in the late eighteenth century, he happened upon a stretch of land that reminded him of a point on the English Channel called Dungeness. When he gave this Washington spit the same name, Vancouver inadvertently established the namesake for what would become one of the Northwest's most iconic foods. The beautiful Dungeness crab was at first known simply as "edible crab" or just "crab." But as the fishery for this delectable, sweet crab became more significant in the early twentieth century, it took on the name "Dungeness." Today the Dungeness crab is one of the foods mostly closely identified with the Pacific Coast.

This is just one of many crab that grace dinner tables and backyard summertime spreads around the country, though. Of them, I know Dungeness best and will, without apology, call it my favorite. But devotion to other crab species runs just as strong elsewhere. In this book I take my love of Dungeness as a starting point and branch out to contemplate a number of crab that contribute to some of the most delicious eating experiences available. Blue crab from the Atlantic and Gulf coasts, stone crab from Florida, and king and snow crab from Alaska: they're all iconic in their own ways.

When it comes to enjoying crab, simple is best for most seafood fanatics: freshly cooked, with melted butter and/or lemon wedges, plenty of napkins, and a crisp, cold beverage. It's hard to imagine ever tiring of that brand of delicious. From this minimalist starting point (see Northwest Crab Boil, page 146), crab proves to be surprisingly versatile in the kitchen. In the shell crab can be boiled, steamed, stewed, roasted, and grilled. The rich, sweet-briny meat adds panache to recipes from breakfast, through lunch (in soups, salads, and sandwiches), into cocktail hour, and finally on the dinner table. I stop just short of making crab ice cream, but trust me, it's out there.

A BRIEF HISTORY

Of the dozens of crab species found in the waters of the Pacific Coast, three contribute most to the commercial and culinary character of the region: Dungeness, king, and snow crab. The latter two are fished primarily in the deep, frigid waters of Alaska, while Dungeness are found from Alaska to California.

The San Francisco Bay area reported some of the earliest commercial activity with Dungeness crab along the Pacific Coast. Early fishing records date back as far as 1848, when Italian settlers to the region began harvesting and selling local fish. This dawning industry grew quickly as the California Gold Rush gained steam, bringing new customers to the region as well as disillusioned prospectors who turned their attention from hopes of gold to heaps of seafood. It is believed that crab were initially an incidental catch—fishermen intending to catch anchovies, sole, or sardines would sometimes find crab trapped in their nets.

By the early 1860s crab were being marketed along the San Francisco waterfront and crabbing had become a more targeted fishery. Early crabbing records farther north on the Pacific Coast don't appear until near the end of the 1800s. Those early commercially harvested crab didn't make it far from the dock where they were landed, though, since there weren't yet systems in place to reliably distribute the perishable shellfish.

It wasn't until the 1920s and 1930s that a more significant crab fishery developed up and down the West Coast, in tandem with advances in refrigeration and processing techniques as well as development of transportation networks. It was about this time too that the name "Dungeness" became attached to the distinctive reddish-purple crab so abundant here. Today the Washington coastal town of Sequim, which grew out of an early settlement on the Strait of Juan de Fuca, embraces the crustaceous critter that shares its name with the nearby Dungeness Spit, the historic New Dungeness Lighthouse, and the Dungeness River that spills out into Dungeness Bay. The Cedars at Dungeness golf course in Sequim even boasts a crab-shaped sand trap they call "Old Crabby" on hole number three.

Substantial domestic commercial harvest of king crab in Alaska wasn't really rolling until the 1940s, though Japanese and Russian fishermen had been catching the crab in good volumes from the north Atlantic the decade prior. By the 1960s American harvest of king crab was dominating, with important operations out of the Bering Sea and around Kodiak Island. This is about the time that commercial harvest of snow crab was just beginning.

Commercial harvest of blue crab goes back well over a century on both the Atlantic coast and in the Gulf of Mexico. Though just as for Dungeness, the crab didn't make it very far from where they were harvested until advances in refrigerated transportation took shape. By the early 1900s that began to change, and the industry became well developed—particularly in the Chesapeake Bay area—in the first half of the century. In more recent decades the commercial harvest has extended down the coast and around into the Gulf of Mexico. Today the top states harvesting blue crab are Maryland, Virginia, North Carolina, and Louisiana.

By contrast to these long-exploited crab, the stone crab industry is a more recent development. Though the crab themselves had been prolific, and caught for subsistence and personal use, for countless generations, early forays into commercial harvest had limited distribution and not great consumer demand. It was later into the 1960s when the fishery and burgeoning market for the claws (beyond what could be consumed at the original stone crab–claw mecca of Joe's Stone Crab in Miami) began to boom.

WEST COAST CRAB

While editor of *Simply Seafood* magazine, I had the rare treat of spending a week on Alaska's Kodiak Island, traditional home to not only the great Kodiak brown bear (of which I got a disarmingly up-close, though safe, view) but also to king crab. A most unforgettable feast during my

visit was prepared by my hosts—seasonal salmon fishing families from the Lower 48 as well as locals from the village of Akhiok at the southern end of the island. The centerpiece in the midst of the salmon pirog (a pastry-topped savory pie), salmon quiche, and salmon pasta salads was a huge bowl of king crab legs, which only hours earlier were still scurrying along the ocean floor. I'd been out in the skiff when the pots were brought up and was absolutely flabbergasted at the sight of those creatures, so big (they can attain up to five feet or more from the tip of one leg to the other) and intimidating with their thorned shells.

Back on shore, a huge pot of seawater was brought to a boil over a propane burner while the crab were cleaned. In no time we were all gorging ourselves on the incredible briny-sweet-rich meat. It was enough to have me swearing off king crab prepared any other way (experiences like that are once in a lifetime, and rightfully so). That was until a more recent development that saw more king crab being transferred live to markets and restaurants in larger cities. Crab are rather sturdy creatures and can survive a day or more out of water in the proper conditions. The king crab are put in large boxes and well chilled, which in addition to preserving the quality of the meat, dulls their senses to keep them docile in transit. Upon arrival at their destination, generally less than twenty-four hours later, the crab go into saltwater tanks and are fully revived. Now it can be possible to enjoy freshly cooked king crab without making that trek to Alaska.

These deep-sea creatures thrive in the frigid waters of the North Pacific, and treacherous ocean conditions there have helped make king crab fishing among the most dangerous professions in the world. Back in the mid-1960s, Kodiak Island was Alaska's largest producer of king crab, landing nearly ninety-one million pounds in 1966. But stocks in those waters declined significantly in the couple decades since peak harvests of Alaska king crab were recorded in the 1980s. Today there is no commercial king crabbing on Kodiak (it's primarily out in the Bering Sea now), but limited subsistence crabbing allowed on the island maintains the tradition.

Red king crab (*Paralithodes camtschatica*) is the most broadly distributed of the major king species, a huge crab that's maroon red when alive, turning bright orange red when cooked. Alaska harvest is from waters that span the Bering Sea, Aleutian Islands, and Gulf of Alaska. The size of red king crab generally ranges from four pounds to ten pounds but can weigh as much as twenty-four pounds. Similar in size is the blue king crab (*Paralithodes platypus*), so named because of the slight bluish hue on the shells in its live state. When cooked, these blue kings turn a similar fiery color as red king crab. A slightly smaller king is the golden (or brown) king crab (*Lithodes aequispinus*), which is fished in deeper waters of the North Pacific. King crab can live long lives, up to thirty years.

Snow crab is the common name that can be attached to two closely related species of crab: *Chionoecetes opilio* and *C. bairdi*. Bairdi, which also sometimes goes by the name tanner crab, are harvested only in Alaskan waters, while the opilio crab are fished also around Newfoundland and Labrador in the North Atlantic. Their common genus, *Chionoecetes*, translates to "snow inhabitant," reflecting their home in those frigid northern waters. Most consumers will just see "snow crab" available, with no distinction made between the species, but that may be changing as the market for the two species evolves. The opilio crab tends to be smaller (about two pounds), bairdi a bit larger (up to five pounds), though they're generally indistinguishable to the untrained eye. Snow crab is often associated with all-you-can-eat buffets or high-volume restaurants, which might make you a little skeptical. When well handled, the meat has a bright, sweet flavor that's quite wonderful.

It's pretty easy to tell the difference between snow and king legs: king crab legs are rounder with sharp, thorny bumps (be careful!), and snow crab legs, aside from being smaller, are flatter with rough but far less spiky shells.

There's little doubt that the premier Pacific Coast crab is the Dungeness. Its Latin name, *Cancer magister*, is a clue to the cultural status this creature holds. The fishery for Dungeness reaches from the Gulf of Alaska down to Southern California. Limited amounts of Dungeness are caught as far south as Santa Barbara, though the bulk of the fishery is from Morro Bay northward. To emphasize how prized this crab is, the Oregon state legislature in 2009 passed a bill naming Dungeness crab the official state crustacean.

WHAT'S IN A NAME?

I had always loved how *Cancer magister* rolls off the tongue, and the regal nature of Dungeness that the name calls to mind. That, and it was among few scientific species names that I knew without hesitation, should I find myself on *Jeopardy!* someday answering a five-hundred-dollar question in the crustacean category. But as I was reviewing notes about Dungeness crab for this book, I was surprised to find many resources that label it *Metacarcinus magister* instead. Despite the fact that the taxonomic change means nothing relative to the cooking and eating experience, I was intrigued. Apparently recent research has determined that what had been a subgenus, *Metacarcinus*, in fact fulfills all the characteristics of a full genus, and therefore scientists elevated it to such status, displacing its longtime *Cancer* genus. Though not all scientists agree—so some, whether out of habit or scientific difference of opinion, continue using *Cancer magister*. You know I'm a fan.

BLUE CRAB

DUNGENESS CRAB

KING CRAB

STONE CRAB CLAWS

SNOW CRAB

EAST COAST CRAB

Two prime crab species that are in commercial production along Eastern Seaboard and Gulf of Mexico waterways are blue crab and stone crab. There is some commercial harvest of peekytoe crab and Jonah crab, though in much smaller volumes and very limited availability relative to the blue or stone.

Blue crab are nearly a religion unto themselves, particularly around the Chesapeake Bay and along Gulf Coast spots where the crab are abundant. Their Latin name, *Callinectes sapidus*, means "beautiful savory swimmer," perfectly reflecting both the look and the deliciousness of the crab. The back two legs of these crab are flat, more like paddles than legs, called swimmerets. They do indeed permit the crab to swim around should they wish, while other crab must content themselves with simply walking along the sea floor. They're most always enjoyed quite simply: steamed or boiled whole with seasonings of choice (a choice about which, also, passions can run deep) and piled on a paper-covered table outside for contented cracking and slurping with lots of friends. After all they sell these crab by the bushel, about forty pounds or so, maybe six to eight dozen depending on their size. (See page 148 for more on crab feeds.)

These are smaller crab than most others, which affords them a unique trait that other crab don't have: that of being delectable (some would say outrageously so) in their soft-shell form. All crab have hard exoskeletons, so the only way for them to increase in size as they mature is to slip out of their shell and produce a new shell one size larger into which they'll grow over the subsequent weeks. When captured at just the right moment—within a window of as little as an hour or two—the thin, nearly translucent shell of a blue crab is fine enough that the crab, once cleaned, can be eaten whole, shell and all. The only caveat is choosing a cooking method that fully crisps that soft shell to make it palatable (it'd be quite tough otherwise), which means either pan-frying or deep-frying. Darn, right?! Check out my recipe for the delicacy on page 95.

The other dominant crab of the eastern United States is stone crab (*Menippe mercenaria* and *Menippe adina*, very closely related and treated as one species by the industry). It, too, has a rather unique characteristic in that only its claws are harvested. And its claws are surely the envy of all other crab in the sea: they can grow inordinately large calling to mind Popeye's disproportionately large arms. The crab can regenerate a lost claw within twelve to eighteen months. Once the claw is removed from the crab, the meat holds up much better in cooked form than raw, so the industry standard is to cook the claws immediately, whether onboard the vessel or right after docking. Stone claws are, therefore, always ready-to-eat and the majority of them are enjoyed chilled, right out of the shell. The classic accompaniment is mustard sauce (of which I have a variation on page 79), though lemon butter, cocktail sauces, and other seafood-friendly dips are good choices too. Though the meat is not often picked from the shells to use in recipes, it certainly makes for a luxurious option in the simplest of recipes in which the crabmeat will stand out.

SEASONAL CRAB HARVEST

The commercial season for Dungeness crab is a long one, extending nearly year-round in various openings up and down the Pacific Coast. December is when one big push hits, with the opening of the ocean

fishery in many areas (typically on December 1, mid-November in some areas). The bulk of the year's catch will come in the first month or two—and higher supply tends to mean lower prices, making it traditionally a good time to splurge on a big crab feed for family and friends. Alaska's Dungeness season, primarily from off Kodiak Island and in Southeast Alaska, begins in the spring and peaks during the summer. These fisheries, coupled with inland commercial harvest from areas such as Washington's Puget Sound, cover quite a lot of the calendar with retail crab supplies, though the volume available (and relative price point) varies through the year. All commercial crab operations taper with molting season, when crab are biologically sensitive and when their shells are less filled with meat, making them less desirable as well. Late fall commercial openings are generally contingent on confirmation by fishery agents that the bulk of crab in a particular district have fully hardened shells.

In addition to the annual fluctuation of supply and prices, there are also longer cycles that see Dungeness crab supplies rise and fall over an average of seven to ten years, though the pattern is anything but consistent. It's true all along the Pacific Coast, where harvests in recent decades might drop by 30 percent from one year to the next, but rebound by even more in another year or two. There seems to be no single reason for this fluctuation, but influences can include climate, predators, and general oceanic conditions. Such is the nature of wild seafood. Given our modern food chain that's been well tailored to fit our love of consistent availability and prices, it can be frustrating to deal with the vagaries of nature for the supply of our favorite delicacies. But the best things in life—like crab at a price that has you calling friends over for a bountiful crab feed—are always worth waiting for.

Up in Alaska, the prized red king crab is fished commercially for just a couple of months in the fall, while other types such as blue and golden may be harvested from winter into spring. Likewise, snow crab species are generally harvested in Alaska from October through winter and spring, while just the opilio crab are also a significant fishery in waters off eastern Canada, where it is fished in the spring and summer.

Blue crab are harvested quite broadly, found in United States waters from Texas, around Florida, and up the Atlantic coast as far as Maine, though prime fishing grounds don't extend much north of Chesapeake Bay. The seasons vary with the harvest area, sometimes dependent on the weather, but generally volumes are highest in the summer months and into early fall. Gulf states such as Louisiana and Florida harvest the crab year-round and help meet demand for the delicious crustacean when seasons slow down to the north.

Stone crab are harvested, almost exclusively in Florida, with a consistent season that runs October 15 to May 15 of each year.

SPORT CRABBING

True crab lovers shrug at whatever the price of crab may be or uncertainty about which store will have the best product. Instead they jump in the car and head to their favorite crabbing spot to harvest some themselves. In fact, it may be that recreational crabbing is on the rise *because* of higher crab prices in the markets. That, and catching your own crab is right up there with hunting for mushrooms and picking berries on a vacant lot, bringing out the hunter-gatherer instincts in us while we collect exquisite food to enjoy.

Recreational crab fishing seasons for the different varieties of crab vary throughout the country and often licenses are required—check with the Department of Fish and Wildlife, or its equivalent, in your area to find out about regulations before you head out.

One friend says that all he needs to stay stocked in Dungeness is "$1.79 worth of turkey meat for bait and an extended lunch break," with his car or kayak pointed in the general direction of Westport, Washington, or to any nearby Puget Sound pier. Others head to their Whidbey Island cabin, another to a family home on Hood Canal. They get all the crab they can eat, and sometimes more, which is why I find myself occasionally rendez-vousing in a Seattle parking lot to take some extra crab off their hands. Why yes, we are spoiled.

While technically recreational harvest is allowed on many parts of the Pacific Coast, ocean conditions can be uninviting, with some estu-aries and other protected spots more conducive to crabbing for fun. The inland waters of greater Puget Sound (including Hood Canal and other offshoots) in Washington State are a plentiful crab habitat that keeps countless sport crabbers happy through the summer months, with price-less beachside crab feeds ensuing. During summer, many commercial fishers have their eyes on salmon up in Alaska and other prize harvest elsewhere. When the casual crowd is ready to pull their boats in for the season, the commercial folks are back and ready to drop their pots.

East and Gulf coasters have a pretty profound devotion to crabbing for blues as well, no doubt about it. My blue-crab correspondent from Delaware said that most people in that area have been doing it all their lives, and that nothing says "summer" in blue-crab country like those signs seen in coastal areas touting "hot fat crab and cold beer." The blue crab is caught in various types of traps or on trot lines onto which bait

is attached. The lines are let out, you sit and have a cold one, then you slowly pull up that line. If a crab's attached to the bait that he's determined to eat, he'll hold on tight as long as the line's drawn in slowly enough. With a net ready to nab the crab as soon as it's visible, the crabber is one count closer to dinner.

Whatever crab they're catching, sport fishers are decidedly enthusiastic about their fishing spot, their bait and gear, and whatever particular rituals and habits they have about the craft of crabbing. And it's an infectious enthusiasm. Some days I wonder if there are enough turkey and chicken necks available for all that go into crab pots and on trot lines to lure in those luscious crab. While, sure, crab are known to be scavengers that will eat pretty much any dead thing they come across on the sea floor—my intel on bait choices found crabbers preferring to lure with fresh meat (chicken or turkey legs or necks) and occasionally seafood, such as salmon or tuna heads and salmon bones. More than one crabber pointed out that they'd rather eat a crab whose last meal was something fresh.

SUSTAINABILITY

Crab is a seafood that you can indulge in with a clear conscience regarding its sustainability, which is to say the health of its populations, environmental impact of its fishery, and how well its harvest is managed. All the domestic harvest of the species featured in this book generally rank well, if not very well, with sustainability watchdogs.

The Dungeness crab, for one, is nearly a poster child for sustainability. The fishery has had a management strategy known as "3-S" in place for decades. This references sex (only males can be harvested), size (a minimum carapace width ensures all males harvested have had at least one season to mate), and seasonality (varies regionally but avoids disturbing crab postmolt when shells are soft and they are biologically vulnerable). In recent years there has been concern about some instances of humpback whales being entangled in pot lines. Though this is generally considered to be a rarity, given the whale's endangered status, it is nonetheless a call to action for the industry to take measures to reduce likelihood of entanglements.

King crab have had some challenges over the years. It was a prolific and very profitable fishery for decades, until a distinct crash in the 1980s that put the brakes on much of the harvest. There had been a kind of Wild West race-for-the-crab derby approach before: the season opened and it was each boat for itself to get as much crab as it could until the season closed. For a long time that worked, until suddenly it didn't. A number of possible factors have been cited for this crash, including limited recruitment (survival of crab larvae) and changes in climate and ocean conditions, though overfishing is also a likely culprit. Tough but crucial limits on harvest and changes in industry practices, such as annually determined quotas limiting how many crab can be caught based on surveys of that year's population, seem to have paid off. In recent years the populations of king crab in Alaska have clearly rebounded. Reports indicate that populations in the Bering Sea are back to levels two to three times what they were in 1985, though rebound in other Alaska waters has been slower to materialize.

Snow crab are deemed to have healthy stocks, risk little harm to the environment or other sea creatures, and are fished under solid management practices. Like for king crab, if authorities have data suggesting lower abundance of snow crab in a given year, they'll reduce the quota sizes to assure enough mature crab remain to support solid populations in the future. Given the inherent cyclical nature of crab abundance, there's sure to be a boom year not long after one that's slim.

Domestic blue crab too are pretty consistently given the green (or at least yellow) light from sustainability monitors. Biologically, the species has a short but fecund life, which contributes a sizeable cohort of juveniles each year though their survival is contingent on everything from weather to predation. Effective management of stocks and other oversight has helped stabilize the fishery that had—particularly in the Chesapeake Bay—some challenging years not long ago. (Blue swimmer crab from Asia, a different species, can show up in US markets. Concerns about less stringent oversight of fishery practices means consumers are generally recommended to check the provenance of the blue crab they're purchasing to ensure it is from a well-managed source.)

Stone crab get high marks for sustainability as well. The fishery is closed five months of the year during prime spawning season, minimum claw size (at least two and three-quarters inches from tip of the immobile half of the claw to the first leg joint) assures harvest from only mature crab, egg-bearing females must be returned to the water with both claws still intact, and it's illegal to harvest whole crab.

The Monterey Bay Aquarium's Seafood Watch program is a particularly good resource to help consumers make informed choices about the seafood they purchase. It's available online, as a great mobile app, and in pocket-size paper guides. Established through the Vancouver Aquarium in British Columbia is Ocean Wise, which evaluates seafood species from around the globe as well. And the Marine Stewardship Council (MSC) supports an elaborate program that certifies sustainable fisheries.

But bear in mind that this is an "opt-in" program. This means a particular fishery organization that hopes to be certified must initiate the process, not to mention budget a good deal of time and money for the review process that's required. Not seeing your favorite seafood on the MSC list does not mean that the fishery is unsustainable.

It pays to do some research about your favorite seafoods, learn more about the regions where they're harvested, the fishing methods used, and what, if any, environmental impact the fishery has in order to make a decision about what you're comfortable eating. It is rarely as easy as a blanket "good" or "bad" about any single seafood species. So many variables come into play, including when, how, and where the seafood is caught. Informing yourself and asking questions of restaurant staff and retail vendors will go far to help you consume seafood with a clear conscience.

SCIENCE SAYS

So, we know that crab is a gastronomic delicacy on our dinner plates. But what is crab's status in the biologist's lab? First, crab are part of a large group of creatures called arthropods—invertebrates with segmented bodies and jointed legs—which includes insects, spiders, and centipedes. Of those subsets, crab are—along with shrimp, lobsters, and crayfish among others—crustaceans. Within that class, crab are designated as decapods, because they have ten legs.

From this point the crab population falls into one of two groups: brachyurans and anomurans. The former are considered to be the "true" crab because, true to decapods, they sport ten visible appendages: four pairs of legs and one pair of claws. Brachyurans include Dungeness, snow, blue, and stone crab. The anomura crab are also technically decapods, though only the claws and three pairs of legs are visible, the fourth set dwarfed and tucked under the back shell edge. Anomuran crab include the glorious king crab, as well as an array of hermit crab, box crab, and the wild-looking heart crab.

WHAT TO DRINK WITH CRAB

Looking for ideas about what to sip alongside your delectable crab? The short answer is crisp white wine, great sparkling wine, or a nice cold beer. Countless aficionados don't stray far from those options, often having long ago picked favorite selections that are near and dear to their crab-loving hearts. There are a number of options within those three categories, where variations abound.

Let's start with wine. I'll draw a pretty sweeping, though perhaps not all that bold, generalization that West Coasters are more in the wine-with-crab camp while in the East they're more likely to be drinking beer. Not because, necessarily, wine is better suited to Dungeness and beer to blues. It has a lot to do with the native wine culture, with Washington, Oregon, and California all producing a slew of crab-friendly options within a short drive of those crab grounds. Wine is a big part of the culinary landscape. Un- (or only moderately) oaked chardonnay, pinot gris, dry riesling, and dry gewürztraminer can be solid contenders for crab.

Chardonnay is grown around the world and produced in myriad styles. For the simplest of crab preparations with few other flavors and ingredients in the mix, lighter chardonnay with a minimum of oak is ideal. But as the dishes become richer, perhaps in fritters or served with a buttery sauce, the more buttery, lush styles of chardonnay that may have more pronounced oak do quite well. Among my (and many others') favorite chardonnays are those made in Burgundy, where the grape takes on a particular elegance and the wines have a rounded, moderate lushness that makes them wonderful alongside crab.

Generally, wines with some body, not too steely-dry and austere, do best with crab. With oysters I want supercrisp, a good dose of acidity, and striking minerality. With crab it goes more toward lush and rounded with lighter acidity and a bit more fruit character to complement the sweeter, richer-tasting (though technically very lean) meat. Albariño, not-too-fruity viognier, and grüner veltliner are among other solid options.

Ahhhhh, Champagne! Not only is it elegant, delicious, and inherently festive, it is also one of the most broadly food-friendly beverages available. And when it comes to crab, the partnership is particularly brilliant. Speaking now of true Champagne from the namesake region of France, winemaking requirements and the natural environment assure wines that have a bright acidity to counterpoint the rich sweetness of crab, along with complexity from the aging process that elevates the flavor of the crab. Vintage Champagne, in particular, has even more character with its minimum of three years' aging, which shifts flavors from the fruit-forward more toward the savory and earthy.

If you think that rosé Champagne is suited only for "ladies who lunch" occasions, think again. The pink color does not reflect girly sweetness, but instead reflects some red wine influence that gives the Champagne more structure and further boosts its food friendliness. In particular, it remains a strong partner for bolder flavors, elevating and complementing spice where other wines may be overpowered by them.

Sparkling wines are made around the world, though in that broader context the variations in style and flavor are just too vast to generalize for crab pairing. I would recommend focusing on those that have bright flavor, moderate acidity, and minimal sweetness. There are worse tasks than sipping a few different sparkling wines with crab to figure out which one you like best.

And beer? No, I wasn't going to forget beer. In fact, philosophically, one might argue that it is an exemplary crab partner given how well beer echoes the casualness of outdoor summer crab feasts. Given the relatively delicate, slightly sweet flavor of most crab, go for a lighter style of beer such as lager, pilsner, or wheat beer (which sometimes goes by hefeweisen). They tend to be low on the hoppy-bitterness scale and have a cheery brightness that complements crab well.

All this being said, beverage pairing is very much to each his or her own. Our palates are incredibly personal; if breaking any pairing "rule" produces a flavor combination that knocks your socks off—all the more power to that partnership.

DIVERSE TASTES

To make all these pairing considerations more interesting, remember that not all crab taste exactly the same, which becomes clearer when you get a chance to taste different varieties side by side. Dungeness is sweet, lightly salty, with a touch of richness; blue is more sea-breeze, delicate, less salty; king is very rich and the briniest of them all; snow can be even more sweet-salty than Dungeness; and stone is quite sweet, with minimal saltiness, and almost meaty. So while there certainly are beverages that pair well with all five, even those slight variations might lead you toward some species-specific preferences as you explore options.

IN THE KITCHEN

BUYING & STORING CRAB

When buying live crab, choose ones that are visibly active. Let the professionals drop their arms into those live tanks, but you get to accept or reject their choices. An added confirmation of quality (in the case of Dungeness) would be a pinch of one of the back legs to be sure it's fully hard. If it gives rather than feeling solid, the crab may still be filling out after its last molt and not in prime form (there will be less meat and it can be on the soft side).

Keep the crab cool in transit, asking for a bag of crushed ice at the seafood counter if it's warm out or if you won't be home right away, and refrigerate the crab as soon as you get home. Live crab need air, so open up the packaging. I like to clear out a vegetable bin for storing crab, to help contain any water draining. Live crab will be somewhat dulled by the chill of the refrigerator, so don't expect them to rummage around much in there. Don't be tempted to keep them in water (even salted) or on ice, which will do more harm than keeping them in open air. It's best to plan cooking live crab the day you purchase them.

For cooked, whole crab, look for those without punctures or other breaks in the shell. The crab should feel heavy in your hand, indicating that it is full of meat. Check that all its legs, especially the claws, are intact. Blue crab are blue and grayish green when alive, Dungeness a purplish-brown color, both turning a vivid orange red when cooked. The orange-red color is a clue for cooked crab that are ready to eat. Though cleaning Dungeness crab is easy, it can get a little messy, so consider asking the fishmonger to clean the cooked crab for you. In some regions cooked Dungeness is available frozen, either whole or in cleaned sections. See below for info on frozen king and snow crab related to choosing and thawing.

Bulk crabmeat should smell sweet and slightly briny. Avoid any crabmeat that looks dried out or has a heavy "fishy" aroma. Cooked crab, whether in the shell or not, will keep for a few days if well chilled, but it will be at its best for flavor and moistness if used within a day or two of buying it. (If buying packaged crabmeat, refer to the label for storage guidelines.) You should never catch a whiff of ammonia smell with crab, either in the shell or picked meat. That's a clear indicator of a product past its prime.

King and snow crab are commonly sold frozen in sections. Carefully check any exposed flesh that's visible: it should be white and not look dried out, which indicates freezer burn or other poor handling. Often the leg portions will be covered in a thin glaze of ice, which is a good thing. These crab are cooked shortly after hitting the docks, then quickly frozen to preserve the quality of the meat (and help assure the meat doesn't cling to the shells), then glazed with ice to protect them, especially from contact with air. Thaw the crab legs in the refrigerator overnight, in a deep pan (such as an oblong baking dish) to catch the water melt.

Blue crab, both hard-shell and soft-shell, are available—depending on the season—in both fresh and frozen form. Selecting and storing hard-shell blue crab require similar criteria to Dungeness. Soft-shell crab are clearly distinct, though a fresh, clean aroma if fresh and lack of blemishes in either state are key factors to look for.

Stone crab claws are available fresh in season and frozen through much of the year. The shells may have been scored by the processor to make cracking easier; otherwise the shells should appear unbroken. They should have a sweet, briny aroma, if any aroma at all. Plan ahead to allow frozen claws time to thaw slowly in the refrigerator, as noted for king and snow.

I generally never recommend that we home cooks freeze seafood in our home freezers. Seafood that's frozen commercially is done so at temperatures far lower than our freezers can attain, and those extra-low temperatures mean quick freezing and formation of very, very small ice crystals. When we put a piece of fish in our home freezer, it takes longer to freeze, the ice crystals that form are larger, and they become like little knives puncturing cell walls of the meat, altering the texture and reducing the flavor quality the crab will have once thawed.

That being said, if you ever find yourself with more delicate, fresh, sweet crabmeat than you can use (which might sound unlikely, but it can happen) the last thing you want to do is throw it away. One friend tipped me off to the freezing-in-milk option, apparently an old fisherman's trick. After picking meat from the shells and removing any shell bits and cartilage, put the meat (I package it in recipe-friendly eight-ounce portions) in a heavy-duty ziplock bag and add just enough milk to cover. Draw out as much excess air from the bag as you can, seal well, and freeze. When ready to use, thaw overnight in the refrigerator, then drain off the milk and squeeze the excess liquid from the crabmeat before using. The quality holds up quite well. You wouldn't want to use this on a crab Louis salad or for crab cocktail, but it's a great option for soup, risotto, quiche, and many other cooked recipes.

IN A CAN

Not all crabmeat is created equal. In fresh form crabmeat may be sold in plastic tubs or bulk at a seafood counter to purchase by the pound. You may also see crab in a can at the seafood counter, which is pasteurized to protect the contents and extends shelf life a bit, but it has no other ingredients added and must be refrigerated.

The shelf-stable canned crab you'll find alongside canned tuna and anchovies in your grocery store is different: it's generally packaged with additives and preservatives. And these products typically rely on crab harvested in Asia, which is often not the most sustainable option. While crabmeat from bulk trays, plastic tubs, and pasteurized in cans with nothing added are all great products to use in these recipes, I am not a fan of using shelf-stable canned crab in its place.

LIVE CLEANING

This is an option for cleaning blue and Dungeness crab that is practiced by some crabbers and the most ardent of crab cooking fanatics. It involves cleaning the crab from its live state, rather than after it has been cooked. There are a few benefits, which include being able to fill a pot with more cleaned, portioned crab than you can whole crab, for more efficiency when cooking lots of crab. It also leaves the meat more pure white and slightly milder in flavor, since the yellowish viscera is not in contact with the body meat unlike when crab are cooked whole. Lastly, whatever seasoning you may be adding to the cooking process will have better access to the exposed meat, and the crabmeat will better absorb those other flavors.

Cleaning crab live is a bit less daunting a task with smaller blue crab, as they're simply easier to manage. To mellow both the crab and the cook before starting, many put the crab in a big bowl of ice water for five minutes or so to dull it a bit and reduce its activity.

I've cleaned live Dungeness at home and it's doable, but messier than cleaning cooked crab and a little unnerving.

Ultimately this cleaning process is the same as the process for cleaning cooked crab: remove the carapace (top shell), remove the apron, pinch away the gills, and clean out the guts. One slight variation some employ is to cut the crab in half from the abdomen side with a large, sharp cleaver while the carapace is intact (definitely not recommended with a chef's knife or a hesitant cook), which immediately kills and halves the crab in one gesture.

For me, live cleaning is a technique best suited to beach cleaning, where aficionados go through the motions in a matter of moments, first removing the carapace, carefully grabbing the claws and legs together in each hand and breaking the crab in half, shaking out the viscera and quickly swishing the halves in seawater to rinse. Much easier to do so outdoors than in our home kitchens.

Top-quality seafood markets with crab in live tanks should be happy to clean the crab for you. Be sure to keep live-cleaned crab cold in transit and cook them within a few hours.

BOILING & STEAMING CRAB

These are the two most basic ways to cook crab. Boiling is often the first step for just-harvested crab, both for commercial processors and for recreational crabbers. Cooking crab just out of the water captures them at peak freshness and makes transporting and storing easier than for live crab. And for purists, that's all the work needed before taking the crab to the table for a feast. Steaming, too, can perform this task for just-caught crab, whether to be eaten right away or stored for two or three days in the refrigerator before using. But steaming can also double as a means to reheat precooked crab for serving warm. Boiling is not recommended for this; some of the crab's delicate flavor would be lost into the hot water while steaming does a better job of preserving it.

You need a big pot to cook whole crab at home, particularly if you're feeding a crowd. When a crab feed is on the menu, consider using a pot as big as twelve to sixteen quarts to get through the volume of crab to keep everyone happy, or have a couple of smaller pots boiling away at the same time. Even for just one or two Dungeness crab or a dozen blue crab, eight quarts in volume will be best. If cooking lots of crab might become a regular habit, consider larger two-piece pots made with just this in mind, either with a large basket that fits snugly inside the pot for easy adding and removing of the crab, or with a shallower lower portion to hold the liquid and seasonings and a larger pot that sits atop it with the crab perched over for steaming.

TO BOIL CRAB: Fill a large pot with water up to a few inches below the top. Add plenty of salt, about one-half cup per gallon of water. Cover the pot and bring the water to a boil over high heat. If boiling a whole live crab, put it in the freezer to chill and make it docile while the water is heating. (The crab shouldn't freeze, so don't leave it in the freezer for more than fifteen or twenty minutes.) When the water's at a full rolling boil, grab the crab securely at the back of the carapace and carefully but quickly slip the crab into the water headfirst. Reduce the heat to medium high so the water's actively gurgling but not boiling over. Cook the crab for eighteen minutes for a two-pound whole crab (a few or less based on other sizes); cook for about ten minutes if using cleaned crab portions or blue crab.

TO STEAM CRAB: Put about three to four inches of water in a large pot and add a collapsible steamer basket to the bottom of the pot. (If you don't have a steamer basket, you could use a few tuna cans with both top and bottom removed.) Cover the pot and bring the water to a boil over high heat. Sedate the crab in the freezer as noted above. When the water's at a full rolling boil, add the crab to the steamer basket, cover, and steam for about twenty-two minutes for whole Dungeness crab, or about fifteen minutes for crab portions or blue crab. Keep an eye on the water level during cooking to be certain that the pot doesn't boil dry; if necessary, add another cup or two of very hot (preferably boiling) water.

Drain the cooked crab in the sink. If serving the crab chilled, put them in a sink full of ice water to cool quickly, then drain well, clean them if not already cleaned, and refrigerate until ready to serve. If serving the crab hot, give them a quick rinse under warm water, clean them, and you're ready to go.

CLEANING & PORTIONING CRAB

Dungeness & Hard-Shell Blue Crab

To clean a cooked crab (see pages 36 to 37 for photos), begin by removing the carapace by inserting your thumb under the edge of the carapace at the back edge and lifting it up and away from the body. If you're a fan of crab butter (see page 39), spoon out the soft, yellowish material and set aside in a small dish. Otherwise, discard it with the remaining innards that are tucked in the body cavity. Turn the crab over, then lift up and remove the small flap of shell known as the apron. (This apron being narrow and fingerlike, by the way, identifies the crab as a male, as it must be for legal Dungeness; on a female crab the apron is more broad and dome-like, which you may see on blue crab.)

Pinch off the feathery gills that are on either side of the body cavity. Break away the mandibles, or mouth parts, that protrude a bit from the front of the shell. Rinse the crab well under cold water. Use a large, heavy knife to cut the body in half where it narrows at the center. If you have a crab cleaned for you at the market, this is what you'll be taking home. And for blue crab this is generally the last step before cooking or serving.

There are two ways to proceed for portioning Dungeness crab, though for a crab feed, you can leave them in these larger portions. One option is to pull the legs away from the body, then cut each body half into two or three pieces. I prefer a different method that leaves some body meat attached to each leg portion. Set the half crab upright on the chopping board with the legs up and the body portion flat on the surface. Using a cleaver or other large sharp, heavy knife, make a swift downward chop between each of the legs (though I'll keep the last two smaller legs together), through the soft shell of the body. Use whichever method appeals to you.

For precooked crab that is to be used in a recipe, lightly crack the shells of the legs so that flavorings from the other ingredients will more easily penetrate the meat. This is also a jump-start for your guests, making it easier for them to get at the meat. Use crab crackers or a wooden mallet and try to avoid crushing the shell into the meat. Ideally, the legs will remain intact.

If you're serving the crab as is, it's ready for the table. Be sure to provide your guests with crab crackers and small seafood forks for removing the meat from the shells. When you get to the big luscious claws, the meat will come out more easily if you first remove the loose claw joint: grab the pincer and bend it backward, pulling it away from the claw. It should come away with a thin membrane that runs down the center of the claw meat. When serving the crab, have a bowl or two on the table for guests to discard shells as they go.

HOW TO CLEAN A CRAB

1. *Lift up and remove the carapace.*   2. *If you're a fan of crab butter, spoon it out and set it aside.*   3. *Turn the crab over and remove the apron.*   4. *Pinch off the feathery gills.*

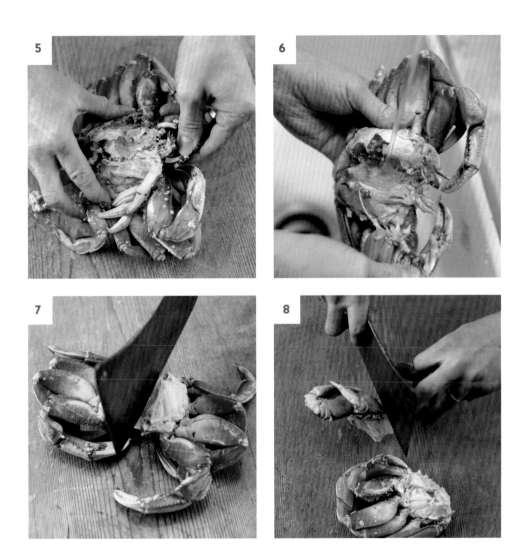

5. *Break away the mandibles.* **6.** *Rinse the crab well under cold water.* **7.** *Use a large, heavy knife to cut the body in half.* **8.** *Set the half crab upright on the chopping board with the body portion flat on the surface. Make a swift downward chop between each of the legs.*

Other Crab

It's pretty rare to come across a king or snow crab live in retail stores—and if you did, think about how big a pot you'd need to cook it once home! King and snow crab are most always precooked, available as individual leg portions or clusters with a few legs together. And they'll likely be frozen as well, so you'll have to thaw the crab overnight in the refrigerator before using (see page 29). From this point there's not much you need to do to clean or portion these crab. Though some legs, particularly king, can be quite long and unwieldy for cooking and serving, so you may wish to cut them in half or thirds before using. If a joint is conveniently located for this, simply bend one side backward to separate it from the other portion at the joint. If not, use a cleaver or a heavy chef's knife to cut through the shell in desired portions.

Note that king and snow crab shells aren't quite as hard as those of Dungeness crab, so crab crackers are less effective to get at the meat. Instead use a pair of slender-bladed kitchen shears to cut down the length of the leg portions and pry apart the shell to expose the meat. Larger poultry-type shears will mangle the meat as they pass down the length of the shells. If you don't have a slender-bladed option, use a heavy, sharp knife to halve the legs lengthwise.

Don't underestimate those spiny protrusions that are particularly pronounced on king crab; they can puncture your skin if you're not careful. You may wish to hold the legs with a kitchen towel or hot pad to grip them securely while you're cutting the shells to avoid hurting yourself.

Soft-shell blue crab are quite distinct from their hard-shell versions, particularly since the shell remains intact through the cooking and eating. But it is important the crab be cleaned before cooking. Some vendors may sell them precleaned, which is a bonus. Lift up one side of the top shell and see if the feathery gills are still intact, which indicates they haven't been cleaned. In this case use your fingers to pinch away the gills from both sides. Then use a pair of kitchen shears to cut away the front portion of the crab body, just about one-half inch behind the eyes and mouth. Flip the crab over and pull up and pinch off the apron flap. Rinse the crab well.

When it comes to stone crab, since only the claws are harvested and they're precooked, you won't need to do much in the way of preparation of this particular crab, aside from a quick rinse under cold water. Since these are some of the hardest crab shells you'll encounter, you're more likely to need a mallet than traditional crab crackers to break through. A small wooden mallet is ideal, but avoid pounding too hard and imbedding

CRAB BUTTER

Crab "butter" is one of those wonderful culinary euphemisms, like sea urchin "roe" (gonads) and "sweetbreads" (thymus gland . . . but oh so delicious!). Also known as tomalley or mustard, this yellow-amber soft material (it's more grayish green when raw) is found clinging to the underside of the carapace and in the body cavity of the crab. It is mostly hepatopancreas, an organ that serves a number of purposes for the crab, which includes acting something like our liver. Devotees of crab butter swear by stirring it into sauces to serve with crab or simply eating it as is. And they like the flavor that it imparts to the adjacent body meat. But others find the flavor too strong, and some agencies don't recommend people consume the crab butter as it's where any toxins harbored in the crab will be concentrated. In fact, some go so far as to recommend that you clean the crab live (see page 31) to remove the viscera before cooking to avoid any potential exposure to toxins or other contaminants.

broken shell into the meat. Each "claw" is really a three-sectioned leg, with two knuckles that have lovely nuggets of meat inside, and the oversized main claw portion. This claw, as for other crab, has a flat piece of membrane that runs down the center of the meat; take care to avoid that when eating.

ABOUT THE RECIPES

Many of the recipes in this book were made with Dungeness crab in mind, simply because it's the prime crab in the Northwest where I've been doing my cooking for a few-plus decades. But as they say, variety is the spice of life, so there's plenty to love about exploring other types of crab. All five types of crab featured in the book are unique characters in terms of size, shape, and flavor. Taken as a whole, these crab offer a broad range of options in the kitchen and many opportunities for some delicious considerations.

A handful of the recipes rely on in-shell crab, in which case the form (claws, legs, a mix) and the size (from small blue crab to huge king crab) have a big impact on how well a particular crab will work in a specific recipe. You'll find that I clarify in the recipes the best options—or possible variations to suit different species—to help steer you in the right direction. When using precooked crab in a recipe the goal is to just heat them through and give them enough time to mingle flavors with other ingredients—too much extra cooking and they'll start to lose their sweet character.

Most of the recipes rely on bulk crabmeat. It's easily the most versatile form for cooking: it's more broadly available than whole crab and allows for more flexibility between the different species. When buying Dungeness meat, you rarely get a choice of meat type; it will generally be a mix of both the flakier body meat and larger pieces of leg meat. Though on rare occasion you may see "fry legs," just the lovely whole nuggets of meat from the larger legs, sold. Blue crab, however, is sold by meat type: jumbo lump (the largest of unbroken pieces from the body), lump (unbroken pieces from the body), backfin or special (remaining body meat, broken lumps and/or flaked meat), and claw meat (smaller pieces tinged reddish brown from the claws).

There are recipes where lump meat is ideal or at least a luxurious option to showcase the premium meat, and I note this in recipes where it's appropriate. Other times its specialness would be lost in a recipe that blends the crab into a batter or stirs it into a soup. In fact in those recipes flake can be ideal because it more readily distributes and blends with the other ingredients. Throughout the recipes I offer notes about what meat type to consider using, though to simplify across species I reference just flake or lump, with the understanding Dungeness customers often don't have a choice. The information will help you lean one way or the other when you do.

Note that some recipes are more crab-forward than others. For instance the Firecracker Crab Cocktail (page 75) is all about the crab with an embellishment of homemade cocktail sauce, while for the Choux Puffs with Curried Crab (page 81), the meat is blended with seasonings and other ingredients for a filling that's not boldly crab-heavy in flavor.

In this way I try to offer a range of crabness to suite different tastes and crowds where perhaps not everyone is a crab fiend. Some recipes offer a range in the amount of crab you could use, so you can embellish that Crab Louis (page 120) more or less luxuriously according to your whim and budget.

In crabmeat recipes I redundantly remind you to pick through the meat to remove shell and cartilage before using it. Small bits of shell tend to stand out visually simply because of their color, but the thin material that surrounds sections of body meat and the strips of cartilage that run down some leg portions are pure white and often hard to see against the white crabmeat. It pays to take an extra few moments to run your fingers through the crab to double check if any hard bits are lingering.

Crabmeat can harbor a lot of liquid, which is a hindrance in some recipes where the added moisture would alter the recipe's results. In those cases I suggest you squeeze the crab gently to remove some of that excess liquid before using it. Just grab a handful and squeeze gently over the sink. In other recipes that liquid is not an issue and in fact melds well with other ingredients.

It's tempting to believe that when you're using a recipe that calls for crabmeat, you'd save money picking the meat yourself from a whole Dungeness crab. But crab economics don't always work out that way. In a rough average I have found that the yield of meat from a whole cooked crab will be about 25 percent of the original weight, though it varies with the thoroughness of picking and with the crab itself—a larger crab will generally have a better meat-to-shell ratio than a smaller one. If your two-pound crab costs eight dollars per pound, that's sixteen

RECIPES

BREAKFAST & BRUNCH

EGGS AND FRESH herbs are, to me, a magical combination of ingredients that play beautifully off each other. Crab is perfectly at home in the mix. This single-serving omelet makes a lovely presentation and is quick enough to make that you'll have two on the breakfast table in no time flat: the perfect tête-à-tête Sunday brunch. The trick to an ideal fluffy omelet is to cook the eggs slowly over moderate heat, so they remain tender and moist. Overheating quickly turns eggs dry and flavorless.

FINES HERBES OMELET WITH CRAB

MAKES 1 SERVING

Crab: any cooked crabmeat, mix of flake and lump ideal

2 large eggs

1 tablespoon water

2 ounces crabmeat

1 tablespoon unsalted butter

½ teaspoon minced fresh chives, plus more for serving

½ teaspoon minced fresh chervil, plus more for serving

¼ teaspoon minced fresh flat-leaf (Italian) parsley, plus more for serving

¼ teaspoon minced fresh tarragon, plus more for serving

1 Crack the eggs into a medium bowl and beat them with a fork until partially blended. Add the water and continue beating until the eggs are evenly blended and a little frothy. Pick over the crabmeat to remove any bits of shell or cartilage. If using king or snow crab leg meat, cut it into small dice. Squeeze the crab gently to remove excess liquid.

2 Melt the butter in a small skillet, preferably non-stick, over medium heat. Add the minced chives, chervil, parsley, and tarragon to the eggs, along with a pinch each of salt and pepper, and stir just to mix. Slowly pour the eggs into the skillet and cook until they are nearly set, 2 to 3 minutes. During this time, slowly draw a wooden spoon across the bottom of the pan in a spiral, starting at the outer edge and working your way to the center, then back out. Keeping the eggs in motion helps them cook evenly. When there is

almost no liquid egg left, stop stirring, scatter the crab-meat evenly over, and cook until the omelet is set, 1 to 2 minutes more.

Kosher salt and freshly ground white or black pepper

Coarsely chopped fresh herbs, for garnish (optional)

3   Take the skillet from the heat. Using a heatproof spatula, fold one third of the omelet toward the center, then fold that center portion again toward the oppo-site edge of the skillet. Carefully roll the omelet from the skillet onto a warmed serving plate. (Ideally, the "seam" will be on the bottom, though it doesn't really matter.) Serve right away, with a sprinkle of chopped herbs across the top if you like.

FINE INDEED

Fines herbes is a French term for the combination of chervil, chives, parsley, and tarragon. Although the blend is commonly available in dried form, for this dish I'd recommend that you use only fresh. Chervil is a delicate herb with lacy, parsley-like leaves and a flavor reminiscent of anise. The herb can be hard to find fresh in markets but is easy to grow, so consider adding it to your kitchen garden or window box. You could use extra chives or pars-ley to replace the chervil if you are unable to find it. If you happen to have any chives blossoming in your garden, pluck the little purple blossoms and scatter some over the omelet for a striking garnish.

SLICES OF TOASTED rustic bread serve as an open-faced foundation on which goat cheese, crabmeat, and vine-ripe tomatoes are layered—a wonderful waker-upper. Mix and match other ingredients to suit your taste and the best of what's available at the market. Add other minced fresh herbs to the goat cheese. When summer's tomatoes are no longer available, you could top the sandwiches with oven-roasted or sun-dried tomatoes, fresh leaves of baby spinach, or a few sprigs of parsley to add a bright finish.

BREAKFAST BRUSCHETTA WITH CRAB & GOAT CHEESE

MAKES 4 SERVINGS

1 Preheat the broiler. Toast one side of the bread slices about 4 inches from the broiler element until lightly browned, 1 to 2 minutes, then turn and lightly toast the other side, 1 to 2 minutes more. Set aside on a wire rack to cool.

2 Crumble the goat cheese into a small bowl and mash it with a fork to soften the cheese slightly. Add the dill with a pinch each of salt and pepper and stir to mix well. Spread the goat cheese mixture over the bread slices.

3 Pick over the crabmeat to remove any bits of shell or cartilage. If using king or snow crab leg meat, cut it into medium dice. Squeeze the crab gently to remove excess liquid. Arrange the crab over the goat cheese. Lay the tomato slices over the crab, garnish with the dill, and serve.

Crab: any cooked crabmeat, lump is luxurious

4 slices country-style bread, about ¾ inch thick

8 ounces fresh goat cheese

1 tablespoon minced fresh dill or other tender herb, plus more for garnish

Kosher salt and freshly ground black pepper

4 to 6 ounces crabmeat

1 large vine-ripe tomato, cored and cut into 8 thin slices

THE SIMPLE GLORY of quiche: when eggs, cream, and cheese combine to cradle ingredients in a flaky crust. Gruyère is the cheese of choice (though Swiss can be used). It's an ideal option for breakfast, brunch, or lunch, or even as an appetizer.

CRAB & LEEK QUICHE

MAKES 8 SERVINGS

Crab: any cooked crabmeat

FOR THE PASTRY DOUGH:

1½ cups all-purpose flour

½ teaspoon kosher salt

½ cup unsalted butter, cut into ¾-inch pieces and chilled

About 5 tablespoons ice water, plus more if needed

———

2 tablespoons unsalted butter

2 large leeks, white and pale-green parts only, split, cleaned, and thinly sliced

Kosher salt and freshly ground black pepper

8 ounces crabmeat

1½ cups grated Gruyère cheese (about 6 ounces)

3 large eggs

1½ cups half-and-half

1   To make the pastry dough, in a food processor, combine the flour and salt and pulse once to mix. Add the butter pieces and pulse to finely chop the butter and create a mixture with a coarse, sandy texture. Transfer the mixture to a medium bowl, drizzle with 3 tablespoons of the water over and stir with a fork to quickly blend. Repeat with the remaining 2 tablespoons of water, stirring well. The dough has the proper amount of liquid if it feels neither dusty-dry nor sticky when you squeeze some between your fingers; stir in a bit more water if needed.

2   Turn the dough out onto a work surface, form it into a disc, and wrap it in plastic. Refrigerate the dough for at least 30 minutes before rolling it out.

3   Melt the butter in a small saucepan over medium heat. Add the leeks and cook, stirring occasionally, until just tender, about 5 minutes. The leeks shouldn't brown; reduce the heat if needed. Season lightly with salt and pepper and set aside to cool.

4   Preheat the oven to 400 degrees F.

5   Roll out the chilled dough on a lightly floured surface to a roughly 12-inch circle, and use it to line a 9- to 10-inch quiche or pie pan. Press the dough gently

dollars. Since you'll get about one-half pound of meat from that crab, you're paying roughly thirty-two dollars per pound for the meat itself. If the price for the bulk meat is in that range, you'll save yourself plenty of time at little or no extra cost buying prepicked meat. Though, on the down side, you won't have crab shells with which to make Crab Stock (page 111). Blue crab have a much lower yield and the crab are so much smaller, I think it's never a debate about buying blue crabmeat versus picking it yourself.

down the sides of the pan to be sure it is evenly covering the bottom. Using kitchen shears or a small knife, trim the outer edge of the dough to a ½-inch overhang, then fold that edge under and use your fingers to flute the pastry edge.

6   Prick the bottom of the shell with the tines of a fork, line the pastry shell with a piece of foil or parchment paper, and add pie weights or dry beans to cover the bottom. Bake the pastry shell until the edges are set, about 10 minutes. Take the pan from the oven, remove the foil and weights, and continue baking the crust until it is lightly browned and the bottom no longer looks raw, 3 to 5 minutes more. (If the bottom of the shell starts to puff up, prick the dough again.) Take the crust from the oven and let cool for about 15 minutes; reduce the oven temperature to 375 degrees F.

7   Scatter the sautéed leeks over the bottom of the pastry shell. Pick over the crabmeat to remove any bits of shell or cartilage. If using king or snow crab leg meat, cut it into medium dice. Squeeze the crab gently to remove excess liquid. Arrange the crab evenly over the leeks and sprinkle the Gruyère over the crab.

8   In a medium bowl, whisk together the eggs to blend, then whisk in the half-and-half with a good pinch each of salt and pepper. Pour the custard over the filling. Bake the quiche until the top is lightly browned and a knife inserted in the center comes out clean, 30 to 40 minutes. Let it sit for about 5 minutes before cutting it into wedges to serve. The quiche can also be served at room temperature, though it needs to be refrigerated if you won't be eating it right away.

WHEN EVERYDAY HASH browns won't do, there is nothing like a dose of gorgeous crabmeat to rise to the occasion. These aren't quite diner-style hash browns, and not trying to be latkes. Somewhere in between, you'll get the crisp crunch of fried potato on the surface, and a tender inside with the pockets of sweet crabmeat throughout. Serve them alongside your favorite egg dish for breakfast or brunch.

HASH BROWN CAKES WITH CRAB

MAKES 6 SERVINGS

Crab: any cooked crabmeat, mix of flake and lump ideal

6 to 8 ounces crabmeat

½ cup finely chopped onion

¼ cup finely chopped fresh flat-leaf (Italian) parsley

Kosher salt and freshly ground black pepper

2 medium russet potatoes (about 1½ pounds)

1 large egg, beaten

Mild olive oil, for cooking

1   Pick over the crabmeat to remove any bits of shell or cartilage. If using king or snow crab leg meat, cut it into medium dice. If any of the other meat pieces are quite large, break them into a few smaller pieces. Squeeze the crab gently to remove excess liquid.

2   In a large bowl, combine the crabmeat, onion, parsley, and a good pinch each of salt and pepper. Stir to mix.

3   Heat a large, heavy skillet over medium heat. Preheat the oven to 200 degrees F.

4   While the skillet is heating, peel the potatoes and coarsely grate them on the large holes of a grater. Grab a good handful of the grated potato and squeeze it well over the sink to draw off excess liquid, then add the potato to the bowl with the crab. Continue squeezing the remaining potato in the same way. When all the potato has been added, add the egg and toss the ingredients well to thoroughly blend.

5   Add about ⅛ inch of oil to the heated skillet. Scoop up about ¼ cup of the potato mixture and carefully add it to the skillet, using a spatula to help form a tidy mound if some of it goes astray. Repeat with more portions of the potato mixture, allowing about 1 inch between the cakes so they're not crowding the pan. Cook the cakes undisturbed until nicely browned on the bottom, 4 to 5 minutes. About halfway through that time, use the flat side of the spatula to press down evenly on each cake to compress it a bit.

6   Turn the cakes over and continue cooking until nicely browned on the other side, 4 to 5 minutes more. Transfer the cakes to a wire rack set on a baking sheet and keep warm in the oven while cooking the remaining potato mixture in the same way. You will likely need to add more oil to the skillet for each batch; they won't brown and crisp well without it. You should get about 12 cakes total.

ALREADY AN INDULGENCE, with its combination of freshly poached eggs and rich hollandaise sauce, this breakfast classic is made even more special when plump crab replaces the traditional ham as a bed for the eggs. Because the crab-egg-hollandaise combination is so rich, I suggest just one muffin half per serving, but for heartier appetites you could serve two. For an extradecadent brunch, you could skip the muffins and crabmeat and use one of the West Coast Crab Cakes (page 141) or East Coast Crab Cakes (page 144) instead as a base for the poached egg and sauce.

Here the hollandaise sauce, traditionally flavored only with lemon juice, gets added flavor from a touch of lemon and orange zest, making the sauce a bit brighter in flavor. It's important to cook the hollandaise sauce over low heat so the egg yolks cook gently and thicken smoothly without becoming grainy. If your burner won't maintain low heat, cook the sauce in a double boiler or in a bowl set over, but not touching, a pan of simmering water.

CRAB BENEDICT

MAKES 4 SERVINGS

Crab: any cooked crabmeat, lump is luxurious

FOR THE HOLLANDAISE SAUCE:

½ cup unsalted butter

2 tablespoons water

2 large egg yolks

1 tablespoon freshly squeezed lemon juice

½ teaspoon finely grated orange zest

¼ teaspoon finely grated lemon zest

1   Preheat the oven to 200 degrees F.

2   To make the hollandaise sauce, melt the butter in a small saucepan over medium-low heat. Once fully melted, use a small spoon to skim off and discard the milk solids that collect on the surface of the melted butter; set aside.

3   In another small saucepan, whisk together the water and egg yolks until blended. Set the saucepan over low heat and cook, whisking constantly, until the mixture has about doubled in volume and is frothy and thick, 5 to 7 minutes.

4 Take the pan from the heat and whisk in the melted butter in a thin, steady stream, leaving behind the milky sediment in the bottom of the pan. Whisk the lemon juice and zests into the sauce, along with salt and pepper to taste. Keep the sauce warm over very low heat or over a pan of hot water.

5 Split and toast the English muffins and set them on a baking sheet. Pick over the crabmeat to remove any bits of shell or cartilage. If using king or snow crab leg meat, cut it into medium dice. Squeeze the crab gently to remove excess liquid. Divide the crabmeat evenly over the muffins and keep them warm in the oven while poaching the eggs.

6 Fill a large skillet halfway with water and add the vinegar. Bring the water to a gentle boil over medium-high heat, then carefully crack the eggs into the water. (To avoid scalding your knuckles, you could first crack each egg into a small bowl, then gently tip the egg from the bowl into the water.) Reduce the heat to medium and simmer gently until the egg whites are set but the yolks are still soft, about 3 minutes. Gently slosh some of the water over the top of the eggs a few times during cooking to help set the surface of the yolks.

7 Scoop out the eggs with a slotted spoon, drain gently on paper towels, and set the eggs on the crab-topped muffins. Set each muffin on a warmed plate, spoon the hollandaise sauce over, and sprinkle with the chervil. Serve right away.

Kosher salt and freshly ground white pepper

2 plain English muffins

4 ounces crabmeat

2 tablespoons distilled white vinegar

4 large eggs

1 teaspoon minced fresh chervil or chives

THIS IS INSPIRED by revisiting the beloved brunch treat, the dutch baby (or German pancake, by which name you may know it). So often served sweetly with powdered sugar and lemon or a fruit topping, this dish can also be savory. It makes quite a glorious presentation with the batter puffed up high and browned around the edges; it's a dish to consider serving from the center of the table, cutting into it only after the initial oohs and aahs have died down. Beyond brunch, this could be cut into smaller pieces and served as an appetizer as well.

There is something magic about the cast iron pan in this recipe. Its dense, heavy construction holds heat with determination and creates a very striking and brown puffy edge for this dish. I've tried it in a less substantial, everyday stainless steel skillet and while the results are delicious and worthy, they're not as dramatic and puffed-crisp around the edges as you'll get from the cast iron pan.

CRAB & MUSHROOM DUTCH BABY

————— MAKES 6 TO 8 SERVINGS —————

1   Preheat the oven to 425 degrees F.

2   Pick over the crabmeat to remove any bits of shell or cartilage. If using king or snow crab leg meat, cut it into medium dice. If any of the other meat pieces are quite large, break them into a few smaller pieces. Squeeze the crab gently to remove excess liquid.

3   Melt 1 tablespoon of the butter in a medium skillet over medium heat. Add the mushrooms and green onion and cook, stirring occasionally, until tender and any liquid given off by the mushrooms has evaporated, 3 to 4 minutes. Transfer the vegetables to a medium bowl and stir in the crab, then stir in the spinach with a good pinch each of salt and pepper (the spinach will wilt slightly, which is the plan).

Crab: any cooked crabmeat, lump is luxurious

6 ounces crabmeat

7 tablespoons unsalted butter, divided

4 large mushrooms (about 6 ounces), wiped clean, trimmed, and diced

¼ cup finely chopped green onion

½ cup moderately packed slivered fresh spinach leaves (see note, page 60)

(CONTINUED)

½ teaspoon kosher salt,
  plus more for seasoning

Freshly ground
  black pepper

4 large eggs

1 cup whole milk

1 cup all-purpose flour

½ teaspoon kosher salt

———

2 tablespoons freshly
  grated Parmesan cheese

4 Put the remaining 6 tablespoons of butter (in one single piece, not cut up) in a 10- to 11-inch cast iron skillet and put the skillet in the oven to preheat while making the batter.

5 Blend the eggs in a blender on high speed for 30 seconds. Add the milk, flour, and salt, then blend for 30 to 60 seconds longer until very smooth and evenly blended.

6 When the butter is fully melted, take the skillet from the oven and gently pour the batter into the center. Scatter the crab mixture over most of the center, leaving the outer 1-inch perimeter of the batter free of crab. Sprinkle the Parmesan over the crab, then return the skillet to the oven and bake until well puffed and nicely browned, 20 to 25 minutes.

7 Set the skillet on a trivet in the center of the table and cut into wedges to serve. Or, simply cut it in the kitchen and serve.

NOTE: To sliver greens such as the spinach here, stack 5 to 6 leaves and roll them up lengthwise in a moderately snug cylinder. Cut across the cylinder to form thin strips, which might range from very thin (known as chiffonade among chefs) to broader strips of an inch thick or more, depending on the use.

IN THIS SAVORY twist on blintzes, the crepe batter contains fresh dill, adding flavor, aroma, and flecks of vibrant green to enclose the rich filling of ricotta with delicate crab. Add some scrambled eggs and fresh fruit, and your day's off to a great start. Two blintzes per person is a substantial brunch main course; if you have a number of other things on the menu, you may prefer to serve one per person. And they'll be delicious as an appetizer course as well. Any extra crepes can be frozen for later use, wrapped well in plastic wrap.

SAVORY CRAB BLINTZES WITH DILL

MAKES 4 TO 8 SERVINGS

1 To make the crepes, in a medium bowl, combine the flour and salt and stir with a fork to mix, then make a well in the center. Break the eggs into a small bowl and beat with the fork just to mix. Add the milk to the eggs and stir to blend. Pour the milk mixture into the well in the flour and begin incorporating the flour just until mixed. Avoid overmixing; the batter may have some tiny lumps, which is fine. Add the melted butter and dill and stir just to incorporate. Cover and refrigerate for 1 to 2 hours before cooking the crepes.

2 Lightly coat an 8-inch crepe pan or medium nonstick skillet with melted butter and heat it over medium heat (I like to use paper towel dipped in melted butter to quickly spread an even coating of the butter). Stir the batter once again to remix it. Add a

Crab: any cooked crabmeat

FOR THE CREPES:

1 cup all-purpose flour

½ teaspoon kosher salt

3 large eggs

1¼ cups whole milk

2 tablespoons unsalted butter, melted and cooled, plus more for cooking the crepes and for baking dish

2 teaspoons minced fresh dill

8 ounces crabmeat

1 (15-ounce) container part-skim ricotta cheese

(CONTINUED)

½ cup small-curd
cottage cheese

2 tablespoons freshly
squeezed lemon juice

2 tablespoons minced fresh
flat-leaf (Italian) parsley

1 teaspoon minced fresh dill

½ teaspoon finely grated
lemon zest

Kosher salt and freshly
ground black pepper

scant ¼ cup of the batter to the pan and quickly but gently swirl the pan so the batter evenly coats the base. Cook the crepe until the surface turns from shiny to dull and the edges are just beginning to curl, about 1 minute. Using a small spatula, carefully flip the crepe and cook on the second side until lightly browned on the bottom, 30 to 60 seconds longer.

3 Transfer the crepe to a plate and continue with the remaining batter, stacking the cooked crepes one on top of the other. It's very common for the first (and sometimes second) crepe to be a total failure, so don't think twice about tossing out early crepes that don't work. You need 8 crepes for this recipe and will have batter enough to make extra (they freeze well, securely wrapped in a couple layers of plastic wrap).

4 Preheat the oven to 350 degrees F. Lightly butter a 9-by-13-inch baking dish.

5 To make the filling, pick over the crabmeat to remove any bits of shell or cartilage. If using king or snow crab leg meat, cut it into small dice. If any of the other meat pieces are quite large, break them into a few smaller pieces. Squeeze the crab gently to remove excess liquid.

6 In a medium bowl, combine the ricotta and cottage cheeses and stir to blend. Stir in the crab, then add the lemon juice, parsley, dill, and lemon zest and stir to blend. Season with a pinch each of salt and pepper.

7 Lay one crepe on the work surface with the more attractive side down. Spoon about ⅓ cup of the blintz filling into the center of the crepe and spread it out a bit to form a rectangle. Fold in the sides of the crepe over the filling, then fold down the top edge, and finally fold the bottom edge up, making a tidy rectangular package.

8 Set the blintz, folded side down, in the baking dish, and repeat with the remaining crepes and filling. Lightly brush the tops of the blintzes with more melted butter and bake until they are heated through, about 20 minutes.

9 Transfer the blintzes to individual plates, serving 1 or 2 per person.

I'M AN ARTICHOKE purist, I guess, finding that prepared artichokes—whether canned bottoms or bottled hearts—are always disappointing compared to their fresh counterparts. For that reason, this recipe starts with a couple of whole artichokes to be trimmed down to the bottoms and simmered. For a shortcut, you can definitely use canned artichoke bottoms; they tend to be smaller than what you'd get from a typical whole fresh artichoke, so use twice as many. You can also use blanched asparagus in place of the artichokes.

CRAB & ARTICHOKE FRITTATA

————— MAKES 6 TO 8 SERVINGS —————

1 Fill a medium bowl with cold water and squeeze the juice from one lemon half into it, dropping the lemon half into the water as well. (If using canned artichoke bottoms, skip to preheating the oven.)

2 Using a small, sharp knife, cut the stem from one artichoke where it meets the base. With your fingers, pick off a few rows of the tough outer leaves (being careful to avoid any thorny tips) until you begin to see the bulbous outline of the artichoke bottom and the leaf bases are more pale than dark green. Using the knife, trim away the tough green skin covering the base and sides of the artichoke bottom. Rub the cut edge of the remaining lemon half over the artichoke to help avoid discoloration. Holding the remaining cone of leaves with one hand, cut away the leaves about ¼ inch above where they meet the artichoke bottom (the fuzzy choke will be removed after the bottoms are cooked). Put the artichoke bottom in the lemon water and repeat with the second artichoke.

Crab: any cooked crabmeat

1 lemon, halved (if using fresh artichokes)

2 large whole artichokes, or 4 canned artichoke bottoms

2 tablespoons unsalted butter

½ cup thinly sliced red onion

6 to 8 ounces crabmeat

8 large eggs

Kosher salt and freshly ground black pepper

(CONTINUED)

3   Bring a medium pan of salted water to a boil over high heat. While the water is heating, cut a circle of parchment or waxed paper to a size about the same diameter as the pan. Add the artichoke bottoms to the boiling water, reduce the heat to medium, and lay the paper circle on the surface of the water. The paper helps keep the artichokes protected from contact with the air. Cook the artichokes until tender when pierced with the tip of a knife, 20 to 30 minutes, depending on their size. Drain the artichokes and run cold water over them to cool quickly; when cool enough to handle, scoop out the choke with a small spoon and discard it. Set the artichoke bottoms aside.

4   Preheat the oven to 375 degrees F.

5   Melt the butter in a medium ovenproof skillet, preferably nonstick, over medium heat. Add the onion and cook, stirring, until it just begins to soften, 3 to 5 minutes. Take the skillet from the heat and spread the onion out evenly over the bottom of the skillet. Cut the artichoke bottoms into ¼-inch slices and arrange them over the onion. Pick over the crabmeat to remove any bits of shell or cartilage. If using king or snow crab leg meat, cut it into medium dice. Squeeze the crab gently to remove excess liquid. Scatter the crab over the vegetables.

6 Whisk the eggs in a medium bowl until well blended, then whisk in a good pinch each of salt and pepper. Pour the eggs gently into the skillet and return it to medium heat until the bottom is set and the edges are beginning to firm up, 5 to 7 minutes. Transfer the skillet to the oven and bake just until the top is set and the eggs are cooked through (no longer jiggly in the center when the skillet is nudged), 5 to 7 minutes more. Slip the frittata onto a cutting board, cut it into wedges, and serve right away.

BREAD PUDDING SHOWS up in a lot of guises these days, making an appearance here at the breakfast table with tangy sourdough bread holding sweet crabmeat in an herby custard. Feel free to use a non-sourdough bread if you prefer.

SOURDOUGH BREAD PUDDING WITH CRAB

MAKES 8 SERVINGS

Crab: any cooked crabmeat

Unsalted butter, for buttering

1 small loaf day-old rustic sourdough bread (about 1 pound), cut into ½-inch cubes, divided

2 cups grated sharp cheddar cheese (about 8 ounces), divided

½ cup minced onion

8 to 12 ounces crabmeat

8 large eggs

3 cups whole milk

2 tablespoons minced fresh flat-leaf (Italian) parsley

1 tablespoon minced fresh chives

Kosher salt and freshly ground black pepper

1   Preheat the oven to 350 degrees F. Generously butter a 9-by-13-inch baking dish.

2   Scatter about half of the bread cubes evenly in the baking dish, and sprinkle 1½ cups of the cheese over the bread, followed by the onion. Pick over the crabmeat to remove any bits of shell or cartilage. If using king or snow crab leg meat, cut it into small dice. Scatter the crab over the onion, then top the crab with the remaining bread cubes.

3   In a medium bowl, whisk the eggs to blend, then whisk in the milk, parsley, and chives with a good pinch each of salt and pepper. Pour the egg mixture over the bread and let sit for about 10 minutes, pressing the cubes down so they evenly soak up the custard.

4   Sprinkle the remaining ½ cup cheese over the top and bake the bread pudding until the top is lightly browned and a knife inserted in the center of the dish comes out clean, about 45 minutes. If the top is well browned before the eggy custard is cooked, loosely cover the dish with a piece of foil. Let the bread pudding sit for a few minutes before cutting it into pieces to serve.

APPETIZERS

FRIED SPRING ROLLS can be addicting for their crispness, but I prefer the unfried version that allows the flavors of individual ingredients to shine more boldly. Fresh herbs and plump crab—with crunch from lettuce and body from cellophane noodles—make these simple spring rolls as easy to enjoy as they are to make. Rice paper wrappers come in brittle, semitranslucent rounds that need to be dampened before using. Look for them in Asian markets or on well-stocked grocery shelves near other Asian products.

FRESH SPRING ROLLS WITH CRAB

MAKES 4 TO 8 SERVINGS

Crab: any cooked crabmeat, lump is luxurious

FOR THE DIPPING SAUCE:

3 tablespoons unseasoned rice vinegar

3 tablespoons freshly squeezed lime juice (from 1 to 2 limes)

1 teaspoon fish sauce, plus more if needed

½ teaspoon minced or pressed garlic

½ teaspoon sugar

½ teaspoon sriracha or other hot chile sauce, plus more if needed

1½ ounces dry cellophane (bean thread) noodles

8 to 12 ounces crabmeat

8 (8-inch) round rice paper wrappers

1 To make the dipping sauce, in a small bowl, combine the vinegar, lime juice, fish sauce, garlic, sugar, and sriracha and stir to mix. Set aside while making the spring rolls.

2 Put the cellophane noodles in a small heatproof bowl and pour boiling water over them to cover. Let soak until tender, about 5 minutes, then drain well and let cool. When cool, cut the noodles into sections about 3 inches long, using kitchen shears or a knife. Don't worry about the evenness of the pieces; you're just making the noodles easier to handle by portioning them a bit.

3 Pick over the crabmeat to remove any bits of shell or cartilage. If using king or snow crab leg meat, cut it into roughly 2-inch sections. If any pieces are quite thick, halve them lengthwise. Squeeze the crab gently to remove excess liquid.

4 Fill a shallow dish, such as a pie pan, with water. Dip one of the rice paper wrappers in the water until evenly moistened, 5 to 10 seconds, and lift it up to allow excess water to drip off. Lay the wrapper on the work surface (it will become fully pliable in less than a minute) and begin layering ingredients on the wrapper, first setting a piece of lettuce horizontally just below the center point. On top of the lettuce, arrange even layers of about one eighth each of the cellophane noodles, carrot, mint leaves, and cilantro leaves, then set one-eighth of the crabmeat on top. Fold the bottom of the wrapper upward over the filling, then fold in each side and roll the package away from you to fully and snugly enclose the filling in a cylinder. Repeat with the remaining wrappers and filling ingredients.

5 Cut each of the spring rolls in half crosswise, at a slight angle, and arrange the halves on individual plates or a platter. Stir the dipping sauce to remix and taste for seasoning, adding a bit more fish sauce and/or sriracha to taste. For individual servings, provide a small dish of dipping sauce for each diner, or leave the sauce in a single bowl if serving from a platter.

8 small green lettuce leaves, rinsed, dried, and halved (ribs discarded)

1 cup coarsely grated carrot

½ cup loosely packed fresh mint leaves

½ cup loosely packed fresh cilantro leaves

HERE'S AN EXAMPLE of "simple is best": no lettuce, no filler, no frills, just crab and good homemade cocktail sauce. You could use three-quarters cup of ketchup rather than both ketchup and chili sauce, though the latter adds more texture to the mix. To be clear, this is old-school tomato-based chili sauce in a bottle, not a hot, peppery sauce.

I like to put a bit of the cocktail sauce in the dish first so that when you get to the bottom you still have some of the zesty sauce for the last of the crab.

FIRECRACKER CRAB COCKTAIL

MAKES 6 TO 8 SERVINGS

1   To make the cocktail sauce, in a small bowl, combine the ketchup, chili sauce, horseradish, lemon juice, green onion, Worcestershire, and hot pepper sauce to taste and stir to mix. Refrigerate until ready to serve. The flavor will be best if it's made at least 1 hour before serving, to allow the flavors to meld, but it can be made up to 2 days in advance.

2   Just before serving, spoon about 1 tablespoon of the cocktail sauce into individual small dishes. Pick over the crabmeat to remove any bits of shell or cartilage. If using king or snow crab leg meat, cut it into medium dice. Divide the crab among the dishes. Spoon the rest of the cocktail sauce over the crab, set the dishes on small plates, and place the lemon wedges on the plates.

Crab: any cooked crabmeat, lump is luxurious; good dip for stone claws

FOR THE COCKTAIL SAUCE:

½ cup ketchup

¼ cup chili sauce

2 tablespoons horseradish, preferably freshly grated

2 tablespoons freshly squeezed lemon juice (from about 1 small lemon)

2 teaspoons minced green onion tops

½ teaspoon Worcestershire sauce

Hot pepper sauce

12 to 16 ounces crabmeat

1 lemon, cut into wedges, for serving

THIS SIMPLE PIZZA recipe has no sauce to speak of, just a brush of extra-virgin olive oil over the dough before it is topped with crab and fresh mozzarella. The peppery crunch of arugula added just before serving makes a delightful finish. And I like the unexpected touch of heat from red pepper flakes too, though that's an optional element. This small, thin-crusted pizza is meant to be served in wedges as a first course or snack, but it could also be served whole as a single main course serving.

Try to find fresh mozzarella for this recipe. You can use firmer, more shreddable mozzarella, though its flavor and texture aren't as luscious as fresh.

CRAB PIZZA WITH ARUGULA & FRESH MOZZARELLA

MAKES 4 SERVINGS

Crab: any cooked crabmeat, lump is luxurious

FOR THE PIZZA DOUGH:

1 cup all-purpose flour, plus more for flouring

½ teaspoon kosher salt

⅓ cup warm water (105 to 110 degrees F)

1 teaspoon active dry yeast

1 tablespoon mild olive oil, plus more for oiling

6 to 8 ounces crabmeat

4 ounces fresh mozzarella, cut into ⅛-inch-thick slices

1 To make the pizza dough, in a medium bowl, stir together the flour and salt, making a well in the center. Pour the warm water into the well and sprinkle the yeast over the water, stirring it into the water gently. Let sit until the yeast is frothy, about 5 minutes. Stir the dough, gently drawing in the flour from the edges and adding the mild olive oil as you go. When the dough becomes cohesive and forms a ball, transfer it to a lightly floured work surface and knead for a few minutes until it becomes smooth and satiny.

2 Put the dough in a lightly oiled bowl (it can be the same bowl you mixed the dough in), and turn it to evenly but lightly coat the dough with oil. Cover the bowl with a clean kitchen towel and set aside in a warm place until the dough has risen by about half, about 1 hour.

3 Preheat the oven to 450 degrees F. (If using a pizza stone, follow the manufacturer's instructions, which generally include preheating the stone with the oven.)

4 Pick over the crabmeat to remove any bits of shell or cartilage. If using king or snow crab leg meat, cut it into medium dice. Squeeze the crab gently to remove excess liquid. Lay the mozzarella slices on a double layer of paper towel to drain. Drawing off excess moisture from the crab and cheese will help keep the pizza from getting soggy.

5 Turn the risen dough out onto a lightly floured work surface and knead it gently. Press the dough into a rough circle and roll it out to about 12 inches across. (If using a baking sheet rather than a pizza stone, roll the dough into a more rectangular shape that will easily fit on your baking sheet.) The dough may start springing back after a bit of rolling. When this happens, let the dough rest for a minute or two before continuing.

6 If using a pizza stone that is preheated in the oven, sprinkle a thin layer of cornmeal on a peel or on an upside-down baking sheet, and lay the dough on top. Otherwise, simply sprinkle the cornmeal on a heavy baking sheet and top with the dough. Brush about 1 tablespoon of the extra-virgin olive oil over the dough, leaving a 1-inch perimeter that is not oiled. Scatter the crabmeat evenly over the oiled dough and lay the cheese slices over the crab, in a random pattern. Sprinkle with the pepper flakes.

Fine cornmeal, for sprinkling

2 tablespoons extra-virgin olive oil, divided

¼ teaspoon dried red pepper flakes (optional)

2 handfuls arugula, rinsed, dried, and tough stems removed (about 1 cup moderately packed)

(CONTINUED)

7 For the pizza-stone bakers, slide the pizza carefully but quickly from the peel onto the preheated stone (manufacturer's instructions should have pointers on this trick). Otherwise, put the baking sheet in the oven and, either way, bake until the crust is firm and the cheese is gently melted, 12 to 16 minutes. Take the pizza from the oven and scatter the arugula leaves evenly on top. Drizzle the remaining 1 tablespoon of extra-virgin olive oil over the arugula, cut the pizza into wedges, and serve.

STONE CRAB CLAWS are a special treat, there's no doubt about it. To showcase the rich-tasting meat, the claws are usually served very simply, often with the longstanding traditional accompaniment of mustard sauce. Given the sweetness of the meat, I thought a subtle dose of peppery horseradish would be a welcome addition to the mustard. Stone crab claws range in size (and price per pound); any claws will work here. About half a pound per person is ideal for an appetizer portion.

For some homemade flair in the sauce I start here with whole mustard seeds, which need to soak for a couple of days before grinding into the sauce. The result is a mustard with a deeper, more peppery mustard flavor. You can certainly skip that step and simply use three tablespoons of Dijon mustard (smooth or grainy) and omit the mustard seeds, water, and vinegar. If using the seeds, finishing the sauce at least a few hours before you plan to serve it will be a good idea, to allow the flavors to meld.

STONE CRAB CLAWS WITH MUSTARD-HORSERADISH SAUCE

MAKES 4 TO 6 SERVINGS

1 In a small bowl, combine the mustard seeds, water, and vinegar and stir to mix. Loosely cover the bowl and let it sit at room temperature until the seeds are plumped and more tender, about 2 days, stirring a few times each day.

2 Drain the seeds from the liquid, reserving both. In a food processor, put the seeds and 2 tablespoons of the liquid (the rest can be discarded) and pulse 10 or 12 times to break up some of the mustard seeds, scraping down the sides of the bowl 2 or 3 times. Add the mayonnaise, sour cream, horseradish, Worcestershire

Crab: made with stone crab claws in mind, but can be a dip for other cooked crab

2 tablespoons yellow or brown mustard seeds (or a blend of both)

2 tablespoons water

2 tablespoons white wine vinegar

½ cup mayonnaise

¼ cup sour cream

(CONTINUED)

1 teaspoon prepared horseradish

½ teaspoon Worcestershire sauce

½ teaspoon kosher salt

2 to 3 pounds cooked stone crab claws, thawed if frozen, shells partially cracked

sauce, and salt. Pulse a few quick times to blend, then process for 30 seconds until well blended, scraping down the sides once or twice. (Refrigerate the sauce if not serving right away.)

3 Transfer the mustard sauce to individual dishes. Arrange the crab claws on plates, with the sauce alongside for dipping.

THIS RECIPE COMES *with a wink and a nod to Trader Vic's restaurants, founded by Victor Bergeron, which helped bring the exotic flavors of the Pacific Islands to the United States during the white-bread era of the mid-twentieth century. I can still remember what an adventure it was to eat at his Seattle restaurant, long closed but once an exotic refuge in the Westin Hotel (originally the Washington Plaza Hotel) downtown.*

The choux *puff recipe will make about twice as many puffs as you'll need, but it's not practical to make in smaller batches. You can either double the filling recipe if you will be serving a crowd, or freeze the extra puffs: once cooled, arrange them on a baking sheet and freeze them until solid, then transfer them to an airtight container to freeze for up to one month. When you're ready to serve them, simply arrange the frozen puffs on a baking sheet and reheat at 350 degrees F before using. It's an outstanding shortcut to have on hand for future cocktail snacks!*

CHOUX PUFFS
WITH CURRIED CRAB

MAKES 4 TO 6 SERVINGS

1 Preheat the oven to 400 degrees F. Line 2 baking sheets with parchment paper or silicone baking mats.

2 To make the *choux* puffs, in a medium saucepan over medium heat, combine the water, butter, and salt and warm until the butter is fully melted. The liquid should not boil; reduce the heat if needed. Add the flour all at once and stir gently with a wooden spoon until fully incorporated. Continue to stir the flour, a bit more vigorously now, until it forms a smooth dough that pulls away from the sides of the pan, about 1 minute longer.

Crab: any cooked crabmeat, flake ideal

1 cup water

½ cup unsalted butter, cut into 1-inch pieces

1 teaspoon kosher salt

1 cup all-purpose flour

4 large eggs

FOR THE FILLING:

1 tablespoon unsalted butter

(CONTINUED)

⅓ cup finely chopped
green onion

1 teaspoon curry powder

6 ounces crabmeat

1 tablespoon dry sherry

Kosher salt and freshly
ground black pepper

½ cup (4 ounces) cream
cheese, softened at
room temperature

¼ cup finely chopped
water chestnuts or celery

3 Take the pan from the heat and add 1 of the eggs. (To help avoid any shell getting into the dough, you can first break the egg into a ramekin or other small dish. After removing any stray shell bits, tip the egg into the saucepan.) As soon as the egg is added, stir well to blend fully into the dough. Add the remaining eggs one at a time in the same fashion, creating a smooth and glossy dough.

4 Spoon the *choux* dough into a pastry bag fitted with a ¾-inch plain tip. Pipe the dough into rounds of about 1½ inch in diameter on the lined baking sheets, with 1 inch between them. (Alternatively, form the dough with two spoons—see Alternative to Piping on the facing page.) The tops of the mounds should be smooth; if there are any peaks, even them out with the back of a spoon or your finger. When one baking sheet is filled, bake until browned and well puffed, about 25 minutes. Shortly before the first tray is done baking, pipe the remaining dough onto the second baking sheet and bake as for the first. Let the *choux* puffs cool for a few minutes on the baking sheets, then transfer them to a wire rack to cool completely.

5 To make the filling, melt the butter in a medium skillet over medium heat. Add the green onion and cook, stirring, until softened and aromatic but not browned, 1 to 2 minutes. Add the curry powder and stir to mix, cooking for about 1 minute longer. Set the skillet aside to cool.

6 Pick over the crabmeat to remove any bits of shell or cartilage. If using king or snow crab leg meat, cut it into small dice. If any of the other meat pieces are quite large, break them into a few smaller pieces. Squeeze the crab gently to remove excess liquid. Add the crabmeat and sherry with a good pinch each of salt and pepper to the curry mixture and stir to mix, then stir in the softened cream cheese and water chestnuts until evenly blended. You can make the filling up to 4 hours ahead and refrigerate; let it come to room temperature before serving.

7   Preheat the oven to 450 degrees F.

8   Use a small serrated knife to halve 16 *choux* puffs and spoon a generous tablespoon of the crab filling into each, topping with its lid. Arrange the puffs on a baking sheet and warm in the oven for 3 to 5 minutes. The filling won't be heated through, just lightly warmed, and the tops of the *choux* will crisp up a bit. Transfer the puffs to a platter and serve.

ALTERNATIVE TO PIPING

It's traditional to use a pastry bag to pipe *choux* dough onto baking sheets, forming tidy little mounds. But if you don't have a pastry bag, don't fret. Use a couple regular spoons, scooping up about a generous tablespoon of the dough in one, and using the other to tidily scrape it onto the baking sheet. Do your best to form neat shapes, though they'll self-correct a bit in the oven.

AS MUCH AS I like sushi, it's not something for which I get a hankering to make at home. Sushi chefs are well-armed with the skills, tools, and wide array of top-quality ingredients at hand that make ordering, rather than making, sushi so fully enjoyable. Chirashi means "scattered"—this home-style sushi is not wrapped in nori but instead served in a bowl with selected toppings. A particular delight is how much room there is for variations, using different toppings and seasonings to suit your taste.

CHIRASHI SUSHI WITH CRAB

MAKES 4 TO 6 SERVINGS

1 In a medium saucepan, combine the rice, 2 cups of the water, and a good pinch of salt. Bring the water to a boil over medium-high heat, then cover the pan, reduce the heat to low, and cook until the rice is tender and the water fully absorbed, about 20 minutes. Fluff the rice gently with a fork, then cover with the lid to keep warm.

2 Put the wasabi powder in a small bowl, add the remaining 2 teaspoons water, and stir to make a smooth paste. Stir in the vinegar, soy sauce, and sugar until well blended.

3 Pick over the crabmeat to remove any bits of shell or cartilage. If using king or snow crab leg meat, cut it across into pieces about 2 inches long; if any of those pieces are quite thick, halve them lengthwise. Put the crab in a medium bowl. Drizzle about 2 tablespoons of the vinegar mixture over and toss to mix; set aside.

4 Transfer the warm rice to a medium bowl and pour the remaining vinegar mixture over, stirring well with the fork to evenly coat the rice. Set aside to cool.

Crab: any cooked crabmeat, lump ideal

1 cup short- or medium-grain rice

2 cups plus 2 teaspoons cold water, divided

Kosher salt

1 to 2 teaspoons wasabi powder

⅓ cup unseasoned rice vinegar

2 teaspoons soy sauce

1 teaspoon sugar

8 ounces crabmeat

2 large eggs

1 tablespoon mild olive or vegetable oil

¼ cup slivered fresh shiso leaves (optional)

2 tablespoons minced peeled ginger

(CONTINUED)

2 ounces daikon
radish sprouts, or
¼ cup coarsely grated
red radish

¼ cup slivered nori
(see note below)

1 tablespoon toasted
sesame seeds

4 to 6 thin lemon slices,
for serving

5 In a small bowl, beat the eggs with a pinch of salt. Heat half of the oil in a medium skillet, preferably nonstick, over medium heat. Add half of the egg mixture and swirl the pan so it evenly coats the base. Cook until set, about 1 minute, then flip the egg over to cook for about 30 seconds on the other side. Transfer the egg to a cutting board and repeat with the remaining egg, setting the second cooked round on top of the first. Let cool, then roll the egg into a loose cylinder and cut across into roughly ¼-inch slices, separating the slices with your fingers.

6 Stir the shiso and ginger into the cooled rice and arrange it in an even layer in the bottom of individual bowls. Scatter the slivers of egg over the rice, followed by the daikon sprouts. Arrange the crab evenly over the sprouts, then form a small mound of the nori slivers in the center. Scatter the sesame seeds over all, add a lemon slice to the side in each bowl, and serve.

NOTE: Nori—thin sheets of dried seaweed—comes in rather large packets that may be quite a lot more than you'd likely get through in other recipes. Thankfully, small toasted (and often seasoned) sheets of nori have become a popular snack item. You may find the snack-size packets of nori that can be used for the slivered nori that is among the rice toppings. I'd opt for the plain type rather than seasoned, though a little sesame flavor would be nice. Kitchen shears will be the easiest way to sliver the sheets, whichever type you use.

THESE FRITTERS HINT at hush puppies; the nuttiness of cornmeal is a tasty complement to the sweet crabmeat. This is ideal for flakier meat that will blend well into the cornmeal batter, though a few larger pieces of meat here and there provide decadent nuggets to bite into. For notes on a manual version of making the aioli, see Making Mayo on page 153.

Temperature control when deep-frying is important, not only for your safety but to assure that the fritters will be cooked through, not still gooey, when the outside is nicely browned. It's best to use a cooking thermometer to keep tabs on the heat level while you're frying. The fritters will be at their best if served right away.

CRAB CORNMEAL FRITTERS WITH LIME AIOLI

MAKES 4 TO 6 SERVINGS

1 To make the lime aioli, in a food processor, combine the egg yolk, lime juice, and garlic and pulse to blend. With the motor running, begin adding the oil, a few drops at a time, until the mixture starts to thicken, showing that an emulsion is beginning to form. Continue adding the oil in a thin, steady stream. When all the oil has been added, add the lime zest, with a good pinch each of salt and pepper, and pulse a few more times to mix evenly. Transfer the aioli to a bowl, cover with plastic wrap, and refrigerate until ready to serve. The aioli will have a more pronounced flavor if made a couple of hours before serving, but let it sit at room temperature for at least 10 to 15 minutes before serving. (Makes 1 scant cup.)

Crab: any cooked crabmeat, flake ideal

FOR THE LIME AIOLI:

1 large egg yolk

1 tablespoon freshly squeezed lime juice

2 cloves garlic, finely chopped

¾ cup mild olive oil

½ teaspoon finely grated lime zest

Kosher salt and freshly ground white pepper

(CONTINUED)

6 ounces crabmeat

Vegetable oil, for frying

½ cup cornmeal

¼ cup all-purpose flour, plus more if needed

1½ teaspoons baking powder

1 teaspoon finely grated lime zest

½ teaspoon kosher salt

⅛ teaspoon freshly ground black pepper

¼ cup whole milk, plus more if needed

1 large egg, lightly beaten

Lime wedges, for serving

2 Pick over the crabmeat to remove any bits of shell or cartilage. If using king or snow crab leg meat, cut it into small dice. If any of the other meat pieces are quite large, break them into a few smaller pieces. Squeeze the crab gently to remove excess liquid.

3 Preheat the oven to 200 degrees F.

4 In a large, heavy saucepan heat about 2 inches of oil (the oil should not come more than halfway up the sides of the pan) over medium heat to about 350 degrees F (use a deep-fry thermometer to check the temperature). While the oil is heating, in a medium bowl, combine the cornmeal, flour, baking powder, lime zest, salt, and pepper and stir to mix. Add the milk and egg and stir to make a smooth batter. Add the crab to the batter and stir to blend evenly. The batter should be moist and firm enough to hold its shape when lifted in a spoon, but not stiff. If on the stiff side, stir in a bit more milk. If too soft, stir in a bit more flour.

5 When the oil is hot enough, scoop up a generous tablespoonful of the fritter batter and use another spoon to transfer it gently into the hot oil. Cook 4 or 5 fritters at a time until they are nicely browned and cooked through, about 3 minutes, carefully turning them once or twice so they cook evenly. Scoop out the fritters with a slotted spoon and drain on a wire rack set on a baking sheet and keep them warm in the oven while cooking the rest of the batter. Allow the oil to reheat as necessary between batches.

6 Arrange the warm fritters on individual plates, spoon some of the lime aioli alongside, and add a lime wedge to each plate. You can also serve the fritters on a platter, with the aioli in a bowl at the center and lime wedges scattered around. Serve right away.

KEEPING WARM AND CRISP

For so long I would drain just-fried foods such as these fritters on a double layer of paper towels or maybe brown paper on occasion. But depending on how moist the food is that's been fried and how long it will be held, the portion touching the paper can get a little humid and lose some of its crisp character, not to mention sit in the draining oil. I'm now more likely to set these just-fried foods on a wire rack instead, which helps preserve the crispness. I have one such rack that fits perfectly within my favorite rimmed baking sheets. This is particularly handy for items to be kept warm in a low (about 200 degrees F or so) oven—one easy unit to handle. To catch oil drips, you can lay some paper towels or brown paper beneath the rack if you like.

IT'S MUCH EASIER to make a soufflé than you may think, and there's nothing quite so impressive when it comes fresh from the oven, all puffed and richly browned. The simple combination of flavors from the corn and crab is quite wonderful, but if you'd like to add herbs, feel free. I'd suggest a couple tablespoons of minced fresh chives, chervil, or parsley. This soufflé could also be served as a light main course.

CRAB & CORN SOUFFLÉ

———— MAKES 4 TO 6 SERVINGS ————

Crab: any cooked crabmeat, flake ideal

3 tablespoons unsalted butter, plus more for buttering

Dry bread crumbs, for coating

6 ounces crabmeat

1 ear tender sweet corn (white or yellow), husks and silk removed

¼ cup all-purpose flour

1 cup half-and-half

1½ teaspoons Dijon mustard

½ teaspoon kosher salt

⅛ teaspoon freshly ground white or black pepper

¼ cup finely chopped green onion

2 large egg yolks

4 large egg whites

1   Preheat the oven to 375 degrees F. Generously butter a 1½-quart soufflé dish and coat it with dry bread crumbs, tapping the dish gently while it's upside-down to remove the excess. Pick over the crabmeat to remove any bits of shell or cartilage. If using king or snow crab leg meat, cut it into small dice. If any of the other meat pieces are quite large, break them into a few smaller pieces. Squeeze the crab gently to remove excess liquid.

2   Trim the stem end of the ear of corn and set it upright on a cutting board. Use a sharp knife to cut downward to remove a few rows of the kernels at a time, turning the ear and repeating until you have cut away all of the kernels. Try to avoid cutting too deeply, so you get mostly tender kernels and not the tougher core. Using the back of the knife, repeat the same motion around the ear again, this time scraping away any of the tender corn still clinging to the core. You should have about 1 generous cup of corn.

3 Melt the butter in a medium saucepan over medium heat. Add the flour and cook until it foams up and smells slightly nutty, stirring often with a whisk, 2 to 3 minutes. Add the half-and-half and whisk to mix well. Continue cooking, whisking often, until well thickened, 2 to 3 minutes more. Whisk in the mustard, salt, and pepper. Transfer the soufflé base to a large bowl and stir in the crabmeat, corn, green onion, and egg yolks. Set aside. (The base can be made a few hours in advance and refrigerated, but let it sit at room temperature for a bit to take the chill off before continuing.)

4 In a medium bowl, using a hand mixer or large whisk, beat the egg whites until moderately stiff peaks form; do not overbeat or they will become grainy. Add one-quarter of the egg whites to the crab mixture and stir to lighten the soufflé base. Gently fold in about half of the remaining egg whites, then fold in the last of the egg whites until thoroughly combined.

5 Pour the soufflé mixture into the prepared dish, smoothing the top a bit. Bake until it is puffed up and nicely browned on top, 35 to 40 minutes. Serve immediately, using two large spoons to scoop out the soufflé onto individual plates.

THIS VARIATION ON the tostada makes great cocktail party fare. The tortilla pieces can be cut and toasted in the morning and then stored in an airtight container after they are fully cooled. Or, for a major shortcut, use good store-bought corn chips in place of the home-toasted tortillas, though the long, slender triangles used here make for a more elegant presentation and are sturdier than many commercial chips. The topping is best made not more than an hour before serving.

CRAB & AVOCADO TOSTADAS

MAKES 6 TO 8 SERVINGS

Crab: any cooked crabmeat

6 ounces crabmeat

1 ripe but firm avocado

3 tablespoons freshly squeezed lime juice (from 1 to 2 limes)

1 tablespoon minced fresh cilantro

½ teaspoon minced jalapeño

Pinch ground cumin

Kosher salt

6 corn tortillas

2 to 3 tablespoons vegetable oil

2 to 3 tablespoons sour cream (optional)

About ¼ cup loosely packed fresh cilantro leaves

1   Pick over the crabmeat to remove any bits of shell or cartilage. If using king or snow crab leg meat, cut it into small dice. Squeeze the crab gently to remove excess liquid. Put the crab in a medium bowl.

2   Peel and pit the avocado, cut it into small dice, and add it to the bowl with the crab. Drizzle the lime juice over the mixture, and use a fork to lightly mash the avocado while gently blending it with the crab. Add the minced cilantro, jalapeño, and cumin, with a pinch of salt. Stir gently to mix and refrigerate until ready to serve. The crab/avocado mixture should be a bit chunky rather than smooth.

3   Preheat the oven to 350 degrees F.

4   Lightly brush both sides of each tortilla with some of the oil. Cut each tortilla in half, then cut about ½ inch from the rounded edge opposite the diameter cut, to square off each half a bit. (These trimmings can

be discarded or toasted with the rest of the tortillas as a snack for the cook.) Halve the tortilla pieces diagonally to make two long, slender triangles, and lay the pieces on two baking sheets.

5   Toast the tortilla pieces in the oven until crisp and lightly browned, about 10 minutes, switching the baking sheets halfway through. Alternatively, you could toast the triangles on one sheet, half at a time. Let the tortilla pieces cool on a wire rack.

6   Just before serving, scoop a spoonful of the crab/avocado mixture onto the broader end of each tortilla chip. Add a tiny dollop of sour cream, and top with a cilantro leaf. Arrange the tostadas on a platter and serve.

AN ABUNDANCE OF fresh herbs create a strong—and very green—foundation of flavor for this sauce, reflecting the verde in its name. You can use other tender herbs that you may have on hand, such as lovage, chervil, or tarragon (though a little tarragon goes a long way so I wouldn't recommend using much of it). The sauce will be most flavorful if it's made at least one hour in advance. This recipe can double as a main course as well, serving two crab per person.

Since soft-shell season is limited to generally the summer months, and the delicate creatures don't travel particularly well in fresh form, many of us will be using frozen, which hold up quite well. Thaw them slowly in the refrigerator overnight, and dry them well before cooking. These will be best fried just before serving to assure the crispest results.

PAN-FRIED SOFT-SHELL CRAB WITH SALSA VERDE

MAKES 4 TO 6 SERVINGS

1 To make the salsa verde, pile together the parsley, green onion, capers, thyme, oregano, and garlic on the chopping board and chop across the pile—back and forth for a minute or so—to more finely chop them and to jump-start melding their flavors together. Transfer the herb mixture to a medium bowl and stir in the vinegar and oil. Season with a good pinch each of salt and pepper and set aside at room temperature, stirring now and then. The salsa will be most flavorful if it's made at least an hour before serving, but it can be made up to 4 hours in advance.

Crab: soft-shell blue crab

FOR THE SALSA VERDE:

⅓ cup chopped fresh flat-leaf (Italian) parsley

¼ cup chopped green onion

2 tablespoons drained capers

1 teaspoon chopped fresh thyme

1 teaspoon chopped fresh oregano

(CONTINUED)

1 teaspoon chopped garlic

¼ cup red wine vinegar

3 tablespoons mild olive oil

Kosher salt and freshly
    ground black pepper

———————

1 large egg

2 tablespoons water

Kosher salt and freshly
    ground black pepper

¾ cup all-purpose flour,
    plus more for sprinkling

4 to 6 soft-shell crab
    (2½ to 3 ounces each),
    cleaned and trimmed
    (see page 38)

½ cup mild olive oil, plus
    more if needed

2 Beat the egg well with a fork in a shallow bowl. Add the water and a good pinch each of salt and pepper and beat until well blended. Spread the flour out on a plate. Sprinkle more flour onto a tray large enough to hold the crab. Dip 1 of the crab in the egg, lifting it above the bowl for a few seconds to allow excess to drip off. Lay the crab in the flour on the plate and use your dry hand to coat it well in the flour, patting to remove excess. Transfer the crab to the tray and repeat with the remaining crab, reserving extra flour.

3 Preheat a large, heavy skillet, preferably cast iron, over medium heat. While the pan is heating, coat the crab once more in flour, patting to remove excess.

4 When the skillet is hot, add the oil and allow it to heat for a few moments. Place the crab (don't crowd the pan; cook in 2 batches if needed) top-side down and cook until nicely browned, 3 to 4 minutes. Turn the crab over and continue cooking until well browned and crisp, 3 to 4 minutes more. Transfer the crab to a wire rack or paper towels to drain.

5 Arrange the hot crab on individual plates, spoon the salsa verde over it, and serve.

THIS IS SIMPLE comfort food at its best, a recipe that can be dressed up for a fancy dinner party (serve with a small mesclun salad, tossed with a sherry vinaigrette) or dressed down for a quick midnight snack (forget trimming the bread, just serve the creamy crab mixture on a piece of toast fresh from the toaster). To garnish it in midcentury style, you could scatter some chopped hard-cooked egg on top just before serving.

SHERRIED CRAB & MUSHROOMS ON TOAST

MAKES 6 SERVINGS

1 Melt 1 tablespoon of the butter in a medium skillet over medium heat. Add the mushrooms and onion and sauté until tender, about 5 minutes. Sprinkle the flour over the vegetables and stir for a minute or two to evenly coat them. Add the half-and-half and cook, stirring often, until the sauce is thickened and well blended, 5 to 7 minutes.

2 Pick over the crabmeat to remove any bits of shell or cartilage. If using king or snow crab leg meat, cut it into medium dice. Add the crab and sherry to the sauce, reduce the heat to medium low, and cook just until the crab is heated through, 2 to 3 minutes. Season the sauce to taste with salt and pepper.

3 Toast the bread and cut each piece in half diagonally, forming 2 triangles. Butter the toast lightly with the remaining 1 tablespoon butter, and lay 2 triangles, slightly overlapping, in the center of each of 6 warmed small plates. Spoon the crab and sauce over the toast, sprinkle the parsley over, and serve right away.

Crab: any cooked crabmeat, mix of flake and lump ideal

2 tablespoons unsalted butter, divided

1 cup thinly sliced mushrooms

½ cup finely chopped onion

2 tablespoons all-purpose flour

1½ cups half-and-half

8 ounces crabmeat

3 tablespoons dry sherry

Kosher salt and freshly ground black pepper

6 slices white bread, crusts trimmed

2 tablespoons minced fresh flat-leaf (Italian) parsley

SOUPS & SANDWICHES

A HANDFUL OF sweet crabmeat is an ideal constrast for the zesty, fresh flavors of the vegetables in this gazpacho-like soup. There's no replacement for the flavor and texture of summer's fresh tomatoes—though really good, ripe hothouse tomatoes are the next best thing. Likewise, fresh corn that's tender and sweet, not starchy, is the best choice. This is the essence of summer in a bowl.

CHILLED TOMATO SOUP WITH CRAB

MAKES 6 SERVINGS

Crab: any cooked crabmeat, lump is luxurious

1 ear tender sweet corn (white or yellow), husks and silk removed

2 pounds vine-ripe tomatoes, cored, seeded, and coarsely chopped

1 large cucumber, peeled, seeded, and coarsely chopped

1 large red bell pepper, cored, seeded, and coarsely chopped

1 cup chopped red onion

½ cup loosely packed fresh flat-leaf (Italian) parsley leaves

¼ cup loosely packed fresh cilantro leaves

3 tablespoons mild olive oil

1 Trim the stem end of the ear of corn and set it upright on a cutting board. Use a sharp knife to cut downward to remove a few rows of the kernels at a time, turning the ear and repeating until you have cut away all of the kernels. Try to avoid cutting too deeply so you get mostly tender kernels and not the tougher core. Bring a small saucepan of salted water to a boil over high heat, add the corn kernels, and cook for 1 minute. Drain the corn, run cold water over it to cool, and drain well; refrigerate until ready to serve.

2 In a food processor, put half each of the tomatoes, cucumber, bell pepper, and onion and pulse until quite finely chopped. Do not thoroughly puree them; you want to keep some texture and crunch. Transfer the mixture to a large bowl and repeat with the remaining vegetables, adding the parsley, cilantro, oil, and garlic to this batch. Stir this mixture into the bowl along with the tomato juice. (Alternatively, you can prepare

the soup in a blender, chopping the vegetables in 4 or 5 batches, though the texture will likely be finer.) Season the soup to taste with hot pepper sauce, salt, and pepper, and refrigerate until ready to serve, at least 1 hour.

3   To serve, taste the soup for seasoning, adding more salt, pepper, or hot sauce to taste. Ladle the soup into chilled soup bowls and sprinkle with the corn kernels. Pick over the crabmeat to remove any bits of shell or cartilage. If using king or snow crab leg meat, cut it into medium dice. Arrange the crab in a small pile in the center of each bowl. Serve right away.

2 cloves garlic, finely chopped

3 cups tomato juice, regular or spicy

Hot pepper sauce (optional)

Kosher salt and freshly ground black pepper

8 to 12 ounces crabmeat

THERE'S NO AROMA quite like the herbal-citrus combination that makrut lime leaves and lemongrass add to this soup. The shells left after a crab feast also infuse the broth with a rich flavor. You can rinse and save the shells and freeze them for up to a month. Or, start with whole cooked crab, using its picked meat for the wonton filling (add any extra to the broth before serving) and the shells for the broth. If you have Crab Stock (page 111) on hand, skip the shells and use it in place of the fish stock and some or all of the water.

LEMONGRASS BROTH WITH CRAB WONTONS

MAKES 4 SERVINGS

Crab: any cooked crabmeat, flake ideal

Cleaned shells from 2 whole cooked Dungeness crab (not including the carapace)

2 carrots, sliced

2 stalks celery, sliced

2 shallots, sliced

10 slices peeled ginger

4 stalks lemongrass, trimmed and sliced

6 makrut lime leaves, cut into slivers

8 to 10 whole black peppercorns

4 cups fish stock or chicken broth

Soy sauce

¼ cup thinly sliced green onion tops

1   Preheat the oven to 400 degrees F. Scatter the crab shells in a baking dish and roast until they are aromatic and lightly browned, 20 to 25 minutes, gently stirring once or twice for even roasting.

2   Transfer the shells to a small stockpot and add the carrot, celery, shallots, ginger, lemongrass, lime leaves, and peppercorns. If any crab juices are baked onto the baking dish, add a cup of warm water and stir to dissolve them, adding the liquid to the pot. Add the fish stock with enough cold water to cover the ingredients by an inch or so (about 2 quarts), and bring just to a boil over medium-high heat. Reduce the heat to medium and simmer until aromatic and some of the color of the roasted shells has been imparted to the stock, about 1 hour.

3   While the broth is simmering, prepare the crab wontons. Pick over the crabmeat to remove any bits of shell or cartilage. If using king or snow crab leg meat,

cut it into small dice. If any of the other meat pieces are quite large, break them into a few smaller pieces. Squeeze the crab gently to remove excess liquid.

4 In a food processor, combine the crab with the green onion, carrot, celery, lemon juice, and soy sauce and pulse a few times to blend and finely chop the mixture, without making a paste. Transfer the filling to a small bowl. Lay the wonton wrappers out on the work surface and place a scant tablespoon of the filling in the center of each wrapper. Dip your finger in a small dish of warm water and use it to lightly dampen the edges of the wrappers. Fold each wrapper in half, corner to corner, pressing out as much air as possible and pinching the edges to seal securely. Bring a large pot of salted water to a boil over high heat.

5 When the broth is done simmering, line a fine-mesh sieve with dampened paper towel or a double-layer of cheesecloth and set it over a large bowl. This is extra-important given there are likely some tiny shell pieces that might pass through the sieve otherwise. Strain the broth through the sieve and discard the shells and vegetables. Rinse out the pot and return the broth to it, then season to taste with soy sauce and keep hot over medium heat.

6 When the salted water comes to a rolling boil, add the wontons, reduce the heat to medium, and simmer until they are just tender, 3 to 5 minutes. Drain well in a strainer and put 4 wontons in each bowl. Ladle the hot broth over the wontons, scatter with the sliced green onion, and serve right away.

FOR THE CRAB WONTONS:

4 ounces crabmeat

3 tablespoons minced green onion

1 tablespoon minced carrot

1 tablespoon minced celery

1 teaspoon freshly squeezed lemon juice

1 teaspoon soy sauce

16 thin square wonton wrappers

CALLALOO COMES IN *many forms throughout the Caribbean Islands. One common thread is often the green leaves of the taro plant or other similar greens, which themselves can go by the name "callaloo." Sometimes cooked quite simply as a vegetable dish, callaloo also shows up as stew or soup preparations that dot the islands.*

Variations abound, often with crab but sometimes using conch or salt cod or no fish at all; other greens, such as Swiss chard or spinach, can easily replace the traditional greens. For a main course option that's more substantial, serve the callaloo over steamed rice or cooked black beans.

CALLALOO

MAKES 6 TO 8 SERVINGS

1 Cut the chard stems from the leaves and thinly slice the stems. Stack 3 or 4 chard leaves at a time, roll them up into a cylinder and cut across into roughly ½-inch strips.

2 Heat a large saucepan over medium heat. Add the bacon and cook, stirring, until the fat has rendered and the bacon begins to lightly brown, about 5 minutes (if there's much more than a couple tablespoons of bacon fat, scoop out the excess). Add the chard stems, onion, garlic, chile, and thyme and cook, stirring occasionally, until the onion and chard stems are tender, 8 to 10 minutes. Add the stock and bring to a boil. Add the chard leaves, a large handful at a time, stirring gently until each addition has wilted before adding the next. Stir in the okra with a good pinch

Crab: any cooked crabmeat, mix of flake and lump ideal

1 bunch (about 12 ounces) Swiss chard, trimmed and rinsed

4 slices thick-cut bacon, cut into ½-inch pieces

1 large onion, finely chopped

2 cloves garlic, finely chopped

1 to 2 serrano chiles cored, seeded, and finely chopped

1½ teaspoons chopped fresh thyme

(CONTINUED)

3 cups Crab Stock
(page 111), fish stock,
or chicken broth

8 ounces okra, cut into
1-inch pieces
(fresh or frozen)

Kosher salt and freshly
ground black pepper

8 to 12 ounces crabmeat

1 (13.5-ounce) can reduced-
fat coconut milk

1 lime, cut into wedges,
for serving

each of salt and pepper. Allow the liquid to return to a boil, then reduce the heat to medium low and simmer until the vegetables are tender and the soup has aromatic character, 20 to 25 minutes.

3   While the soup is simmering, pick over the crabmeat to remove any bits of shell or cartilage. If using king or snow crab leg meat, cut it into medium dice.

4   Stir the crab and coconut milk into the soup and simmer for about 5 minutes, until well heated. Taste the soup for seasoning, adding salt or pepper to taste. Ladle the soup into individual bowls and serve right away, with lime wedges on the side for squeezing into the soup.

THIS RICH RECIPE is in honor of Whiskey Flats at Dungeness Spit, the tidal flats at the Dungeness River delta below the bluffs where the town of Dungeness was first settled. The name is derived from an entrepreneurial spirit who was selling bootleg whiskey there long ago. If making crab stock for this recipe, the roasted version will be particularly delicious with its more pronounced flavor.

WHISKEY CRAB SOUP

MAKES 6 SERVINGS

Crab: any cooked crabmeat

2 tablespoons unsalted butter

1 cup finely chopped onion

3 tablespoons all-purpose flour

4 cups Crab Stock (page 111) or fish stock

8 ounces crabmeat

2 cups half-and-half

¼ cup whiskey, plus more for serving

Kosher salt and freshly ground white pepper

2 teaspoons chopped fresh chives

1 Melt the butter in a medium saucepan over medium heat. Add the onion and cook, stirring occasionally, until tender and aromatic, 3 to 5 minutes (the onion should soften but not brown). Sprinkle the flour over the onion and continue cooking, stirring until evenly coated, 30 to 60 seconds. Slowly pour in the crab stock and bring just to a boil, stirring often. Reduce the heat to medium low and simmer until the soup is slightly thickened, stirring occasionally, 5 to 7 minutes.

2 Pick over the crabmeat to remove any bits of shell or cartilage. If using king or snow crab leg meat, cut it into small dice. If any of the other meat pieces are quite large, break them into a few smaller pieces. Add the crab, half-and-half, whiskey, and a good pinch each of salt and pepper to the soup, stirring to blend. Simmer just until the soup is heated through, about 5 minutes.

3 Ladle the soup into individual warmed bowls, scatter the chives evenly over, and serve right away, passing a small pitcher of extra whiskey at the table, for diners to add a final splash to taste if they like.

THIS VIBRANT GREEN pea soup is beautifully accented with a delicate crab mousse that is subtly flavored with fresh mint. If you're using shell peas, the general rule of thumb is that one pound in the pod will produce one cup shelled peas, so you'll need four pounds of in-shell peas. If using frozen peas, look for the "petite" variety, which tends to be more tender and flavorful than larger frozen peas.

Try to use white body meat to avoid creating a muddy color when the crabmeat is pureed. For a shortcut you can skip making the mousse and instead just toss the crabmeat with the minced mint and mound it in the center of the soup. And if you are using blue crab claw meat, that's recommended as well.

PEA SOUP WITH CRAB MOUSSE

MAKES 4 SERVINGS

Crab: any cooked crabmeat, flake ideal

FOR THE CRAB MOUSSE:

5 ounces crabmeat

1 large whole egg

1 large egg white

2 tablespoons heavy cream

1½ teaspoons minced fresh mint

Kosher salt and freshly ground white pepper

———

2 tablespoons unsalted butter, plus more for buttering

1 cup finely chopped onion

1   To make the mousse, pick over the crabmeat to remove any bits of shell or cartilage. If using king or snow crab leg meat, cut it into medium dice. If any of the other meat pieces are quite large, break them into a few smaller pieces. Squeeze the crab gently to remove excess water.

2   In a food processor, pulse the crab a few times to chop it up a bit, and then add the whole egg and egg white and pulse to form a smooth puree, scraping down the sides a few times to ensure that the ingredients are well mixed. Add the cream and pulse to mix. Transfer the puree to a small bowl and stir in the minced mint with a pinch each of salt and pepper. Refrigerate the mixture for about 1 hour.

3 Preheat the oven to 350 degrees F. Lightly butter 4 (¼-cup) ramekins or other small ovenproof dishes (you can use larger ramekins, though the mousse will be shallower and will need a bit less cooking time).

4 Spoon the crab mousse mixture into the ramekins and set them in a baking dish. Add boiling water to the baking dish to come about halfway up the sides of the ramekins. Bake the mousse until it pulls away from the sides of the ramekins and is firm to touch, 20 to 25 minutes.

5 While the mousse is baking, prepare the soup. Melt the butter in a medium saucepan over medium heat. Add the onion and cook, stirring, until tender and aromatic, 3 to 5 minutes. Stir in the peas, and then add the stock. Bring the liquid just to a boil, reduce the heat to medium low, and simmer for 10 minutes.

6 Using an immersion blender or in batches in a food processor or blender, puree the soup until smooth. Return the soup to the saucepan, stir in the half-and-half and minced mint, and season to taste with salt and pepper. Gently reheat the soup over medium heat.

7 When the mousse is cooked through, carefully lift the ramekins from the baking dish and unmold the mousses upside down onto a plate. Ladle the soup into 4 warmed shallow soup bowls, set a mousse in the center of each bowl, and garnish the mousse with the slivered mint.

4 cups freshly shelled peas or frozen petite peas

4 cups Crab Stock (page 111), fish stock, or chicken broth

½ cup half-and-half

2 teaspoons minced fresh mint

1 teaspoon slivered fresh mint

ONE BENEFIT OF that effort you put into picking crabmeat from the shell is not only the luscious, sweet meat, but the leftover shells that harbor wonderful flavor. They're used in Lemongrass Broth with Crab Wontons (page 102) to boost the flavor of fish stock for an Asian-inspired soup. The shells can be used to make a basic stock as well, simmered in water with aromatic vegetables, creating flavorful liquid that's ideal for seafood-based soups and stews. Use only crab shells that have been cooked very simply, without added seasonings. The carapace, or large top shell, should be discarded; use only shells from legs and body for the stock. For an extra dose of flavor, the shells are roasted before simmering, which brings out a richer, slightly nutty/toasty character that subtly enhances the flavor of the resulting stock, although you can skip this step.

CRAB STOCK

MAKES ABOUT 8 CUPS

1 Preheat the oven to 400 degrees F. Scatter the crab shells in a baking dish and roast until they are aromatic and lightly browned, 20 to 25 minutes, gently stirring once or twice for even roasting. Transfer the shells to a stockpot. If any crab juices are baked onto the baking dish, add a cup of warm water and stir to dissolve them, adding the liquid to the pot. (Alternatively, if not roasting the crab shells, put them directly into the stockpot.)

2 Add the onion, celery, thyme, bay leaf, and peppercorns to the crab shells with enough cold water to cover the ingredients by an inch or so (about 3 quarts), and bring just to a boil over medium-high

Crab: cooked crab shells (not including carapace) from Dungeness, king, snow, or blue crab

1½ to 2½ pounds crab shells, rinsed

1 cup coarsely chopped onion

2 stalks celery, preferably with leaves, sliced

2 or 3 sprigs fresh thyme

1 bay leaf, preferably fresh

8 to 10 whole black peppercorns

(CONTINUED)

heat. Reduce the heat to medium and simmer until aromatic, about 1 hour. The water should just bubble lightly rather than roil; reduce the heat if needed. After it's done simmering, take the pot from the heat and let cool to room temperature, which allows more time for the flavors to be drawn from the ingredients.

3 Line a fine-mesh sieve with dampened paper towel or a double layer of cheesecloth. This is extra-important given there are likely some tiny shell pieces that might pass through the sieve otherwise. Set the sieve over a large bowl, slowly pour the stock through it, and let drain. Discard the shells and vegetables and set the stock aside to cool. Any extra stock can be frozen for 2 or 3 months.

TRADITIONALLY, CLUB SANDWICHES have three slices of bread each, but I've modi-fied the idea to a conventional two-slice sandwich in which crab meets up with smoky bacon, sliced tomato, crisp lettuce, and—one of my favorite sandwich embellishments—slices of rich avocado. There's nothing not to like about this sandwich. Just take care to toast the bread only lightly so it doesn't become too crunchy. Old-fashioned white bread is typical for such a sandwich, but you can use any variety you like.

CRAB CLUB SANDWICH

MAKES 2 SERVINGS

1   Lightly toast the bread in a toaster and let it cool. Spread ½ tablespoon of the mayonnaise on one side of each bread slice. Top 2 of the pieces of bread with the lettuce leaves.

2   Pick over the crabmeat to remove any bits of shell or cartilage. If using king or snow crab leg meat, cut it in lengths equal to the width of the bread slices, then cut those pieces lengthwise about ⅜ inch thick. Arrange the crabmeat evenly over the lettuce leaves and squeeze the lemon wedges over the crab, being careful to remove any seeds that might fall from the lemon. Lay the tomato slices over the crab and top with the bacon. Peel, pit, and thinly slice the avocado, and lay the slices over the bacon. Top with the remaining bread (mayo side down), cut each sandwich in half diagonally, and serve right away.

Crab: any cooked crabmeat, mix of flake and lump ideal

4 slices sandwich bread (white, wheat, sour-dough, or other favorite bread)

2 tablespoons mayonnaise

2 large or 4 small leaves green lettuce, rinsed and dried

6 to 8 ounces crabmeat

½ lemon, cut into 2 wedges

4 beefsteak tomato slices, about ⅜ inch thick

4 slices thick-cut bacon, fried crisp

½ ripe but firm avocado

AS AN ALTERNATIVE to standard sandwiches, these could be served open-faced on halved or quartered pieces of bread, each topped with a bit of watercress. Or, for more cocktail-like nibbles, you could serve the crab mixture atop toasted baguette slices or crackers. Even better, scoop a bit of the salad into the slender, delicate leaves of Belgian endive, one of the world's perfect edible containers.

GREEN GODDESS CRAB & WATERCRESS SANDWICH

MAKES 4 SERVINGS

1   In a medium bowl, combine the mayonnaise, green onion, anchovy, parsley, chives, vinegar, and tarragon with pepper to taste. Stir to evenly mix, and refrigerate for at least 1 hour to allow the flavors to blend. (The mixture can be made up to 1 day in advance.)

2   Pick over the crabmeat to remove any bits of shell or cartilage. If using king or snow crab leg meat, cut it into small dice. Squeeze the crab gently to remove excess liquid. Add the crab to the mayonnaise mixture, stir with a fork to mix evenly, and then spoon the crab salad in an even layer on 4 of the bread slices. Top the crab with the watercress leaves, followed by the remaining bread slices. Cut each sandwich in half diagonally and serve right away.

Crab: any cooked crabmeat, flake ideal

½ cup mayonnaise

2 green onions, minced

2 anchovy fillets, finely chopped

2 tablespoons minced fresh flat-leaf (Italian) parsley

1 tablespoon minced fresh chives

1 tablespoon tarragon vinegar or white wine vinegar

1 teaspoon minced fresh tarragon

Freshly ground black pepper

8 ounces crabmeat

8 slices white bread

2 ounces watercress, rinsed, dried, and tough stems removed

WHAT'S NOT TO love about luscious, sweet crab all melty and warm with really good cheese? This recipe was inspired by a specialty at the Bait House Café in Seattle's Ballard neighborhood, the seafaring heart of the city. You could, in fact, buy bait at the Bait House, and, while sitting there eating your crab sandwich, look out over the mouth of the ship canal and watch boats—from pleasure craft to part of the Alaska fishing fleet—saunter by on their way to or from the Hiram M. Chittenden Locks. It was a gloriously Seattle-funky little spot, but sadly is no more.

CRAB & CHEDDAR MELT

MAKES 4 SERVINGS

Crab: any cooked crabmeat, mix of flake and lump ideal

4 slices sourdough bread

12 ounces crabmeat

2 cups grated sharp cheddar cheese (about 8 ounces)

¼ cup thinly sliced green onion

4 to 5 tablespoons mayonnaise

1   Preheat the broiler. Toast one side of the bread slices about 4 inches from the broiler element until lightly browned. Set aside on a wire rack to cool. Keep the broiler on.

2   Pick over the crabmeat to remove any bits of shell or cartilage. If using king or snow crab leg meat, cut it into small dice. Squeeze the crab gently to remove excess liquid. In a medium bowl, combine the crab, cheese, and green onion. Toss to mix, and then add just enough mayonnaise to hold the crab and cheese together; if you add too much, the sandwiches will be soft and weepy. Stir the mixture very well to be sure the ingredients are well blended and cohesive.

3   Spread the crab mixture on the untoasted side of the bread slices and set them on a baking sheet. Broil the sandwiches until the cheese is melted and the top is bubbly, 3 to 4 minutes. Transfer the sandwiches to individual plates and serve right away.

SALADS

JUST WHO THE "Louis" is who inspired this classic no one seems to know for certain, though legend leans toward San Francisco as this salad's birthplace. The legacy lives on and this time-honored recipe needs no updating. To do so would make it not a Louis but instead just another crab salad. The lettuce must be crisp, bright iceberg, the eggs hard cooked, the tomato cut in wedges. Embellish with artichoke bottoms or blanched asparagus, if you like.

And yes, the dressing is at its best made with prepared chili sauce or ketchup, to honor the dishes retro roots. For homemade mayonnaise, you can use the Lemon Mayonnaise recipe (page 152), omitting the lemon zest and using only one teaspoon of lemon juice. Though they are non-traditional options, I'll admit that blue cheese or green goddess dressing would be delicious on this salad as well.

CRAB LOUIS

MAKES 4 SERVINGS

Crab: any cooked crabmeat, lump ideal

FOR THE LOUIS DRESSING:

¾ cup mayonnaise, preferably homemade

⅓ cup chili sauce or ketchup

3 tablespoons finely chopped green onion

1 tablespoon minced fresh flat-leaf (Italian) parsley

Dash Worcestershire sauce

Dash hot pepper sauce

1   To make the Louis dressing, in a small bowl, combine the mayonnaise, chili sauce, green onion, parsley, Worcestershire, and hot pepper sauce and stir to mix. Season to taste with salt and pepper and refrigerate until ready to serve. The dressing will be best if made at least an hour in advance, allowing the flavors to meld.

2   On 4 chilled plates, arrange beds of a couple of the larger lettuce leaves. Cut the remaining lettuce into ½-inch strips and pile them evenly in the center of each plate. Pick over the crabmeat to remove any bits of shell or cartilage. If using king or snow crab leg

meat, cut it into pieces about 1 inch long. Arrange the crab over the shredded lettuce, then add the egg and tomato wedges evenly around the crab, on the lettuce base. Spoon a bit of the Louis dressing over the crab, passing the rest separately.

Kosher salt and freshly ground black pepper

———

1 head iceberg lettuce, cored, leaves separated, rinsed, and dried

8 to 12 ounces crabmeat

4 eggs, hard-cooked, peeled, and quartered (see Hard-Cooked Eggs)

2 small tomatoes or 4 plum tomatoes, cored and quartered

HARD-COOKED EGGS

Technically, eggs shouldn't be "hard-boiled," the high heat of boiling producing whites that become tough and rubbery. Just a gentle simmer is better, or even better yet is the method where you remove the eggs from the heat and let the eggs sit in the water to avoid overcooking them. This is how I prefer to hard-cook eggs: Put the eggs in a pan with enough cold water to cover them by about 1 inch. Put the pan over high heat and bring *just* to a boil. Take the pan from the heat, add the lid, and set aside for 15 minutes. Drain the eggs and chill in a bowl of ice water until cold.

SOBA NOODLES ARE a foundation of Japanese cuisine, their distinctly nutty flavor coming from the buckwheat flour used to make them. In this recipe the noodles soak up a flavorful dressing to serve as a base for crab and crisp vegetables. This salad makes a delicious light main course, particularly on a hot summer's day, or serve it alongside a simply grilled piece of fish—salmon would be a particularly good partner.

CRAB & SOBA NOODLE SALAD

MAKES 4 TO 6 SERVINGS

Crab: any crabmeat, mix of flake and lump ideal

FOR THE SESAME-SOY DRESSING:

⅓ cup unseasoned rice vinegar

¼ cup freshly squeezed lemon juice (from about 1 large lemon or 2 small lemons)

2 tablespoons mild olive or vegetable oil

2 tablespoons soy sauce

2 tablespoons mirin

2 teaspoons toasted sesame oil

8 ounces soba noodles

8 to 12 ounces crabmeat

1 large carrot, peeled and julienned

1 Bring a large pot of generously salted water to a boil over high heat for cooking the noodles.

2 While the water is heating, make the dressing. In a small bowl, combine the vinegar, lemon juice, olive oil, soy sauce, mirin, and sesame oil and whisk to blend. Set aside.

3 When the water comes to a rolling boil, add the noodles and cook just until tender, about 5 minutes. Drain the noodles in a colander and run cold water over to cool the noodles. Drain again well and put the noodles in a large bowl. Rewhisk the dressing and drizzle about three-quarters of it over the noodles, tossing to coat them evenly. Cover the bowl and refrigerate for at least 1 hour, stirring once or twice. (The noodles will soak up the dressing as they sit.)

4 Just before serving, pick over the crabmeat to remove any bits of shell or cartilage, and set aside some larger pieces, if there are any, for garnishing the salad. Add the rest of the crab to the noodles along with the carrot, cucumber, cilantro, and sesame seeds. Toss to mix evenly, and arrange the noodle salad on individual plates. Scatter the green onion over the salad, drizzle with the remaining dressing, and top with the reserved crabmeat.

1 medium cucumber, halved, peeled, seeded, and thinly sliced

¼ cup chopped fresh cilantro

2 tablespoons toasted sesame seeds

¼ cup thinly sliced green onion tops

IT'S JUST A handful of ingredients, but this simple combination tastes quite grand. Butter in salad dressing may sound a little odd, but if you're a fan of brown butter, you'll find the surprise pretty tasty. You can certainly use olive oil in place of the butter if you prefer.

CRAB & GREEN BEAN SALAD WITH BROWN BUTTER DRESSING

MAKES 4 TO 6 SERVINGS

Crab: any cooked crabmeat, mix of flake and lump ideal

1 pound green beans, trimmed and rinsed

6 to 8 ounces crabmeat

8 ounces cherry tomatoes, halved if large

FOR THE BROWN BUTTER DRESSING:

¼ cup unsalted butter, cut into 4 to 6 pieces

¼ cup freshly squeezed lemon juice (from about 1 large lemon or 2 small lemons) or 3 tablespoons red wine vinegar

Kosher salt and freshly ground black pepper

2 to 3 tablespoons coarsely chopped fresh herbs (flat-leaf parsley, chives, chervil, tarragon)

1 Bring a large pan of salted water to a boil over high heat. Prepare a large bowl of ice water. Add the green beans to the boiling water and cook until just barely tender and bright green, 2 to 3 minutes. Drain the beans and transfer them directly to the ice water to cool quickly and avoid overcooking. When cool, drain well and scatter on a kitchen towel to dry while preparing the rest of the salad.

2 Pick over the crabmeat to remove any bits of shell or cartilage. If using king or snow crab leg meat, cut it into medium dice. In a large bowl, combine the drained green beans, crab, and cherry tomatoes and let sit at room temperature while making the vinaigrette.

3 To make the dressing, melt the butter in a small skillet over medium heat. Once melted, continue cooking until the solids have turned a medium brown and smell nutty, 2 to 3 minutes more. Transfer the brown butter to a medium bowl, being careful to scrape out the flavorful browned bits from the bottom of the skillet. Let it cool to nearly room temperature, then add the lemon juice with a good pinch each of salt and pepper. Blend with a small whisk or fork and taste for seasoning, adding more salt or pepper to taste.

4   Drizzle the dressing over the salad. (If the butter has solidified a bit before you dress the salad, set the bottom of the bowl in a pan of warm water and stir until the dressing has softened and the consistency is smooth). Toss well to mix, then arrange on individual plates. Scatter the herbs over and serve.

THE AROMATIC CITRUS flavor of oranges and subtle anisey crunch of fennel make for a great start to any meal, particularly when the briny sweetness of crab is added to the mix. In larger servings this salad makes a light lunch.

Blood oranges are, as their name suggests, a variety of sweet orange that has reddish tones in the flesh that can range from a smattering of red speckles to a solid ruby red. They are available sporadically, and not all markets carry them. Winter into early spring is generally the best season for finding them. Navel oranges, while less colorful, will provide great results as well.

SHAVED FENNEL SALAD WITH CRAB & BLOOD ORANGES

MAKES 2 TO 4 SERVINGS

1 Cut both ends from one of the oranges, just to the flesh. Set the orange upright on a cutting board and use the knife to cut away the peel and pith (the white part under the peel), following the curve of the fruit. Try not to cut away too much of the flesh with the peel.

2 Working over a medium bowl to catch the juice, hold the peeled orange in your hand and slide the knife blade down one edge of a section, cutting it from the adjacent membrane. Cut down the other side of the same section and let it fall into the bowl. (Pick out and discard any seeds as you go.) Continue for the remaining sections, turning the flaps of the membrane like the pages of a book. Squeeze the juice from the membrane core into the bowl. Repeat with the second orange.

Crab: any cooked crabmeat, mix of flake and lump ideal

2 blood oranges or
  navel oranges

1 large fennel bulb

4 green onions, thinly sliced

¼ cup mild olive oil

2 tablespoons red
  wine vinegar

Kosher salt and freshly
  ground black pepper

6 to 8 ounces crabmeat

(CONTINUED)

3 Trim the root end and stalks of the fennel bulb, reserving some of the feathery fronds. Cut the bulb in half lengthwise and cut out the tough core. Using a mandoline slicer or a large, sharp knife, cut the fennel lengthwise into very thin slices, and put them in the bowl with the orange segments. Mince enough of the fennel fronds to measure 1 tablespoon, reserving 4 of the remaining fronds for garnish, and add the minced fennel to the bowl along with the green onion. Drizzle the oil and vinegar over the mixture and season to taste with salt and pepper.

4 Pick over the crabmeat to remove any bits of shell or cartilage. If using king or snow crab leg meat, cut it into medium dice. Add the crab to the salad and toss gently to avoid breaking up the orange pieces. Arrange the salad on chilled plates, drizzling the juices from the bottom of the bowl evenly over the salads. Top with the reserved fennel fronds and serve.

IT IS RATHER luxurious to take exquisite stone crab claw meat from its shell to mix into a salad. But there are times when such a daring move has delicious results. Exotically sweet mango, crisp and juicy jicama, vibrant radicchio—they all play beautifully together as a foundation for the crab. The yield of meat from stone crab is roughly one-third, so you'll need about one and one-half pounds whole claws for the meat needed here. Smaller, and less expensive, medium- or large-size claws will be just fine.

If it is simply anathema to you that the stone crab meat be mixed into the salad, you could instead serve the claws intact as usual and serve the salad alongside as an accompaniment. Save some of the dressing to offer in a small dish for optional dipping of the claw meat.

STONE CRAB & MANGO SALAD WITH CHIPOTLE DRESSING

MAKES 4 TO 6 SERVINGS

1 To make the dressing, in a medium bowl, combine the lime juice, chipotle, and lime zest with a good pinch of salt and whisk to mix. Whisk in the oil to blend. Set aside.

2 Pick over the crabmeat to remove any bits of shell or cartilage. Break up larger pieces of claw meat (knuckle nuggets can remain whole) into 2 or 3 smaller pieces. Avoid finely shredding it; there should still be nice lump portions.

3 In a large bowl, combine the mango, radicchio, and jicama and toss to mix. Whisk the dressing to remix and taste for seasoning, adding a bit more salt

Crab: stone crab or other cooked crab-meat, lump ideal

FOR THE CHIPOTLE DRESSING:

3 tablespoons freshly squeezed lime juice (from 1 to 2 limes)

½ teaspoon minced chipotle en adobo or ¼ teaspoon dried chipotle powder

¼ teaspoon finely grated lime zest

Kosher salt

⅓ cup mild olive oil

(CONTINUED)

if needed. Add half of the crabmeat to the salad and drizzle the dressing over. Toss lightly to mix, then arrange the salad on individual plates. Top with the remaining crab and serve right away.

SMOKY-HOT CHIPOTLE

Chipotle chiles are jalapeños that have been dried and smoked, creating a uniquely rich flavor that's spicy balanced with earthy. They're available as whole dried chiles, in ground form, and en adobo, which is canned in a rich red sauce. In that latter form they're plump and ready to use. A little goes a long way, particularly in a recipe like this where its character is intentionally subtle. Even the smallest cans will have much more than needed here. But the chipotle en adobo will keep well (transferred to a sealed jar) in the refrigerator for a couple of weeks, or they can be frozen for a few months.

8 ounces stone crab
claw meat

1 mango, peeled, seeded,
and cut into about
¾-inch cubes

1½ cups thinly shredded
radicchio

1½ cups peeled julienned
jicama

THE SHARP FLAVOR of raw onion turns sweeter when roasted, making a wonderful base for this tangy vinaigrette dressing. The rich crab toasts finish this spinach salad with a touch of luxury. It makes a great main course for a lunch or light supper, though it could also be served in smaller portions as a starter salad.

SPINACH SALAD WITH CRAB TOASTS & ROASTED ONION VINAIGRETTE

MAKES 4 SERVINGS

Crab: any cooked crabmeat, flake ideal

1 cup coarsely chopped onion

4 tablespoons mild olive oil, divided

4 ounces crabmeat

6 ounces cream cheese, softened at room temperature

Kosher salt and freshly ground black pepper

12 baguette slices, about ½ inch thick

¼ cup red wine vinegar

1 large bunch spinach (about 1 pound), rinsed, dried, and tough stems removed

1   Preheat the oven to 375 degrees F.

2   Put the onion in a small baking dish and drizzle 1 tablespoon of the oil over it, stirring to evenly coat. Roast the onion until tender and lightly browned, about 30 minutes, stirring once or twice to help it roast evenly.

3   While the onion is roasting, pick over the crabmeat to remove any bits of shell or cartilage. If using king or snow crab leg meat, finely chop it. Squeeze the crab gently to remove excess liquid. In a medium bowl, combine the crab and cream cheese. Mix with a fork until evenly blended, and then season to taste with salt and pepper.

4   When the onion is finished roasting, set it aside to cool. Preheat the broiler.

5 Arrange the baguette slices on a baking sheet and toast them about 4 inches from the broiler element until lightly browned. Take the baking sheet from the oven, turn the slices over, and top the untoasted side of each with the crab mixture, mounding it slightly in the center. Return the sheet to the oven and continue broiling until the crab mixture bubbles and is lightly browned, 2 to 3 minutes. Turn off the oven and keep the toasts warm on a lower rack in the oven.

6 Put the cooled onion and its roasting oil in a food processor or blender and puree until smooth. Add the vinegar with the remaining 3 tablespoons oil. Puree to blend, and then season to taste with salt and pepper.

7 Put the spinach leaves in a large bowl, tearing any large leaves in half or thirds. Drizzle the onion vinaigrette over and toss to evenly coat. Arrange the spinach on individual plates and top each with 3 crab toasts.

THE FRESH FLAVORS of asparagus, peas, and herbs are an ideal complement in flavor and color to nutty farro and sweet crabmeat in this easy salad. The recipe is also great with other grains, such as rice or quinoa—you'll need about two and one-half cups of cooked grain. You can certainly serve this salad right away, but the flavor will be even better if it sits for an hour or two before serving.

SPRING FARRO & CRAB SALAD

MAKES 4 TO 6 SERVINGS

Crab: any cooked crabmeat, mix of flake and lump ideal

3 cups water

½ teaspoon kosher salt

1 cup farro

6 ounces asparagus spears, trimmed (halved lengthwise if thick)

1 cup freshly shelled peas or frozen petite peas

6 to 8 ounces crabmeat

3 tablespoons minced fresh flat-leaf (Italian) parsley

2 tablespoons minced fresh basil

⅓ cup mild olive oil

3 tablespoons white wine vinegar, plus more to taste

Kosher salt and freshly ground black pepper

1 In a small saucepan, combine the water and salt and bring to a boil over high heat. Stir in the farro, reduce the heat to medium low, and cook until the farro is tender, 25 to 30 minutes. Drain the farro well and put it in a large bowl. Set aside to cool.

2 Trim 2 inches of the asparagus tip from each spear, then cut the rest of the spears into 1-inch pieces.

3 Bring a medium saucepan of salted water to a boil over high heat and fill a medium bowl with ice water. Add the asparagus pieces to the boiling water and blanch until bright green and just barely tender, 2 to 3 minutes. Scoop out the asparagus with a slotted spoon and put it in the ice water to cool.

4 Return the water to a boil, add the peas, and cook for 1 to 2 minutes. Drain the peas, add them to the ice water, and let cool completely. Drain the vegetables and scatter them on a kitchen towel to dry.

5 Pick over the crabmeat to remove any bits of shell or cartilage. If using king or snow crab leg meat, cut it into medium dice. If any of the other meat pieces are quite large, break them into a few smaller pieces. Add the crab, asparagus, peas, parsley, and basil to the farro.

6 In a small bowl, combine the oil and vinegar with a good pinch each of salt and pepper. Whisk to blend, then pour the dressing over the salad, stirring gently to mix evenly. Set the salad aside for at least an hour if possible. (The salad can be made up to 4 hours in advance; refrigerate if holding for more than 1 hour. Allow it to sit at room temperature before serving.)

7 Taste the salad for seasoning, adding more salt, pepper, or vinegar if needed, then spoon the salad onto individual plates and serve.

THE FRESH CRUNCH and flavor of cucumber and daikon radish make this an exceptionally refreshing salad, similar to the cucumber sunomono often served at the start of a Japanese meal. Lump crabmeat will make the most of the contrast between the sweet, meaty crab and the crisp, vinegary vegetables.

The thin skin and innocuous seeds of English cucumber make it the best choice for this recipe. If you find Japanese cucumber, that would be a natural choice as well. If using a regular cucumber, peel it and scoop out the seeds from each half before slicing.

CUCUMBER & DAIKON SUNOMONO WITH CRAB

MAKES 4 TO 6 SERVINGS

Crab: any cooked crabmeat, lump ideal

1 large English cucumber, halved and thinly sliced

1 small daikon radish (about 8 ounces), peeled and thinly sliced

½ small sweet onion, cut into thin julienne

¾ cup unseasoned rice vinegar

1½ teaspoons sugar

1 teaspoon kosher salt

6 to 8 ounces crabmeat

5 to 6 fresh *shiso* leaves, cut into thin julienne

1   In a large bowl, combine the cucumber, daikon, and onion, and toss to mix.

2   In a medium bowl, combine the vinegar, sugar, and salt. Let sit for a few minutes, then stir the dressing until the sugar and salt have dissolved. Pour the dressing over the vegetables, toss well, and set aside for 15 minutes, so they absorb some of the dressing, stirring a few times. (If the vegetables sit too long, they will lose some of their crispness; the salad is best made shortly before serving.)

3   Pick over the crabmeat to remove any bits of shell or cartilage. If using king or snow crab leg meat, cut it into medium dice.

4 Drain the dressing from the vegetables into a small dish, then add the *shiso* to the vegetables and toss to mix. Arrange the vegetables on individual chilled plates, and top with the crabmeat. Drizzle some of the reserved dressing over each salad and serve.

SHISO

Shiso, sometimes known as perilla, is an herb related to mint and basil that is commonly used in Japanese cuisine. Its vivid green leaves, with their distinctly toothed edges, are also a common garnish on plates of sushi and sashimi. (There is also a purple *shiso*; its flavor is a little milder than the green *shiso*.) The subtle anise-mint flavor adds a wonderful herbal quality to the salad, though you could use mint in its place.

MAIN COURSES

THE RECIPE FOR success when it comes to crab cakes is pretty simple: it's all about the crab. Other ingredients should simply help hold the cakes together and offer the slightest hint of color or flavor contrast. These can be served as an appetizer as well, with one cake per person. For an elegant sandwich serve the cakes on a small bun slathered with the rouille, or make bite-size cakes and top with a dollop of rouille for a cocktail party treat.

Rouille (which means rust *in French) is a rich sauce often served with bouillabaisse. It's quite a garlicky sauce as well; if you prefer less-bold garlic flavor, use just one or two garlic cloves.*

WEST COAST CRAB CAKES WITH ROUILLE

MAKES 4 SERVINGS

1   To make the rouille, roast the red pepper over a gas flame or under the broiler until the skin blackens, turning occasionally to roast evenly, about 10 minutes total. Put the pepper in a plastic bag, seal securely, and set aside to cool. While the pepper is cooling, tear the bread into pieces, put it in a small bowl, and pour the milk over it; set aside to soak.

2   When the pepper is cool enough to handle, peel away and discard the skin. Remove the core and seeds, and coarsely chop the pepper. Put the pepper in a food processor with the garlic and pulse to chop finely. Squeeze the excess milk from the soaked bread and add the bread to the food processor with the egg

Crab: made with Dungeness in mind but other cooked crabmeat can be used; king or snow should be chopped

FOR THE ROUILLE:

1 small red bell pepper

1 slice white bread, crusts removed

½ cup whole milk

3 cloves garlic, crushed

1 large egg yolk

2 teaspoons white wine vinegar

(CONTINUED)

Pinch dried red
pepper flakes

Kosher salt

¾ cup mild olive oil

———

1 pound Dungeness
crabmeat

About 3 cups fresh bread
crumbs (see Fresh Bread
Crumbs, opposite page),
divided, plus more
if needed

2 large egg whites or
1 large whole egg,
beaten

¼ cup minced celery

2 green onions, minced

2 tablespoons minced fresh
flat-leaf (Italian) parsley

Mild olive or vegetable oil,
for frying

yolk, vinegar, pepper flakes, and a generous pinch of salt. Process until smooth, scraping down the sides a couple of times. With the motor running, add the oil in a slow, steady stream. Transfer the rouille to a bowl and taste for seasoning, adding more salt if necessary. Refrigerate until ready to serve; the sauce will thicken slightly when chilled. (Makes about 1½ cups.)

3   To make the crab cakes, pick over the crabmeat, removing any bits of shell or cartilage. Squeeze the crab gently to remove excess liquid. In a large bowl, combine the crab, 1 cup of the bread crumbs, the egg whites, celery, green onion, and parsley and stir to evenly mix. Form the mixture into 8 (3-inch) cakes, pressing the cakes firmly so that the mixture holds together. The mixture should be a bit on the loose side, to best showcase the crab. But if the cakes aren't holding together well, stir in a bit more of the bread crumbs. Lightly coat each side of the cakes with the remaining 2 cups bread crumbs and set aside on a tray coated in more bread crumbs. The cakes will hold together better if they sit in the refrigerator for an hour or so before cooking.

4   Heat about ⅛ inch of oil in a large, heavy skillet over medium heat. Fry the crab cakes (don't crowd the pan; cook in batches if needed) until nicely browned and heated through, 4 to 5 minutes on each side. Transfer the cakes to a wire rack, adding more oil to the pan if needed for another batch. Serve the crab cakes warm, with the rouille on the side.

FRESH BREAD CRUMBS

Dried bread crumbs are a pantry staples that can be readily at hand any time, but here I recommend using fresh bread crumbs instead. They take just a few moments to make and contribute a much lighter texture to the finished cake than dried crumbs would. You'll need about 10 to 12 slices of standard white sandwich bread for the 3 cups of crumbs needed here. Tear the bread into pieces, put them in a food processor, and pulse until it has all been transformed into fine, fluffy bread crumbs.

THE BETTER THE crab you begin with, the better your cakes will be. The very best crab cakes that you'll taste in Baltimore or other crab-serious spots in the East will be large pieces of lump blue crabmeat held together almost mysteriously by as little as possible, the sweet meat easily giving way when prodded with your fork. It doesn't get much better than that. If you can't find all exquisite lump meat, try to find meat that at least has a nice mix of both flaked and larger meat portions. These cakes can be served as an appetizer as well, with one cake per person. For homemade mayonnaise, you can use the Lemon Mayonnaise recipe (page 152), omitting the lemon zest and using only one teaspoon of lemon juice.

EAST COAST CRAB CAKES WITH OLD BAY TARTAR SAUCE

MAKES 4 SERVINGS

Crab: made with lump blue crabmeat in mind but other cooked crabmeat can be used; king or snow should be chopped

FOR THE OLD BAY TARTAR SAUCE:

1 cup mayonnaise, preferably homemade

¼ cup finely chopped cornichon or dill pickle

1 tablespoon white wine vinegar

1 tablespoon coarsely chopped drained capers

1 teaspoon Old Bay seasoning

1   To make the tartar sauce, in a small bowl, combine the mayonnaise, cornichon, vinegar, capers, and Old Bay seasoning and stir well to blend. Refrigerate until ready to serve, preferably for at least an hour to allow the flavors to blend and develop. (Makes about 1¼ cups.)

2   To make the crab cakes, put the crushed crackers in a food processor and pulse until finely ground. Add the Old Bay seasoning and pulse a couple times to blend. (You should have about ½ cup crumb mixture.)

3   Pick over the crabmeat to remove any bits of shell or cartilage. Squeeze the crab gently to remove excess liquid. Put the crabmeat in a large bowl and add the crumb mixture, egg, and Worcestershire sauce.

Use your hands or a spoon to lightly but thoroughly blend the mixture. Set aside for 15 minutes, then form the mixture into 8 (2½-inch) cakes, pressing the cakes firmly so that the mixture holds together. The cakes will hold together better if they sit in the refrigerator for an hour or so before cooking.

4   Heat about ⅛ inch of oil in a large, heavy skillet over medium heat. Fry the crab cakes (don't crowd the pan; cook in batches if needed) until nicely browned and heated through, 4 to 5 minutes on each side. Transfer the cakes to a wire rack, adding more oil to the pan if needed for another batch. Serve the crab cakes warm, spooning a bit of the sauce alongside and serving the rest separately.

12 saltine crackers, coarsely crushed

1 teaspoon Old Bay seasoning

1 pound blue crabmeat

1 large egg, lightly beaten

½ teaspoon Worcestershire sauce

Mild olive or vegetable oil, for frying

PICKER OR PILER?

The world of crab eaters can be split into two distinct groups: pickers and pilers. The pickers enjoy the fruits of their labor as they go, while pilers are those who get all the hard work done first and then hedonistically relish the big heap of ready-to-eat meat when the work's complete. I, for one, am a picker too eager to enjoy the luscious meat to wait. In fact most people I know are pickers. The occasional piler I share a crab feast with ends up doubling his workload to include fending off the rest of us, protecting his precious stash. Surely this picker/piler phenomenon could make an interesting thesis subject for some budding psychologist.

UNLIKE OUR COMPATRIOTS *in the eastern regions of the country, Northwesterners typically add no spice (beyond salt) to the pot when boiling crab for a feast. Having grown up here, of course I adhere to the practice, finding the flavor of the crab itself is near perfection. Some crab lovers simply scoop up clean sea water, which is clearly quite salty, in which to cook the crab. To replicate this at home use water that's been well salted (about ½ cup salt per gallon of water).*

Depending on your guests' appetites and what else you're serving for dinner, the serving size can range from a half crab to a whole crab per person. If you're increasing this recipe to serve a bigger crowd, keep in mind that you'll need a much bigger pot, or plan to cook the crab in batches. See page 148 for more on crab feeds.

NORTHWEST CRAB BOIL

MAKES 2 TO 4 SERVINGS

Crab: made with Dungeness in mind, but live blue crab could be used

2 uncooked Dungeness crab (about 2 pounds each), live or cleaned and portioned (see page 34)

2 large lemons, cut into wedges, for serving

½ cup unsalted butter, melted, for serving

1 Bring a large pot (at least 8 quarts) of generously salted water to a boil over high heat. While the water is heating, put the live crab, if using, into the freezer to dull their senses a bit. (The crab should be well chilled but should not freeze at all, so don't leave them in the freezer for more than 15 to 20 minutes.) When the water's at a full rolling boil, if you're using live crab, grab each of them securely at the back of the carapace, and gently but swiftly drop them headfirst into the boiling water. If you're using cleaned crab portions, simply add them to the boiling water.

2   When the water comes back to a boil, reduce the heat to medium high so the water's gently bubbling but not boiling over. Cook the crab for about 18 minutes for whole, about 10 minutes for cleaned portions, counting from the time that the crab were added to the pot.

3   Drain the crab well. If you cooked portioned crab, arrange the pieces on a large serving platter with lemon wedges around the edges. If you cooked whole crab, clean and portion them (see page 34) before serving. Pour the melted butter into individual dishes for each diner, and serve the crab while still warm.

TO FEED AND TO FEAST

On the West Coast we go nuts for crab feeds, while on the East Coast it's all about crab feasts.

Bring up the topic of "pinnacle Dungeness experience" and most people on the Pacific side will tell you about crab-feed traditions with family and friends: the Thanksgiving or Christmas Eve dinner table that is always piled high with freshly steamed crab or the summer ritual of gathering at the beach house to eat your fill of just-caught Dungeness. Countless public crab feeds are held up and down the Pacific Coast each year, from community fundraisers to school reunion festivities.

By one longstanding tradition, many Dungeness crab feeds are held in the late fall/early winter when the newly opened commercial season generally means good stocks of crab and some of the lowest prices of the year. That's truest for those counting on buying, rather than catching, their crab. For the recreational crabber it's more about summer: extralong daylight, warm temperatures, kids out of school, trips to the shoreside cabin, a compulsion to be outdoors. Western crab feeds have more than one season.

Not only is crab simply a delicious thing to eat on such occasions, there's something socially engaging about dining crab-feed style. For one, all pretense of formality is left at the door. It's a roll-up-your-sleeves-and-eat-with-your-hands extravaganza that puts everyone on an even playing field. Most crab feeds dispense with tablecloths and nice napkins. Instead, hosts cover the table with newspapers (comics or crossword puzzle in view, if you like, for dinnertime entertainment) and offer plenty of paper napkins or paper towels. You're at the table for a good while, rhythmically cracking the shells, picking out the meat, and relishing each bite, with intermittent swigs of beer or wine and forkfuls of coleslaw. This is gastronomic communal interaction at its very best.

Over on the East Coast, however, similar blue crab indulgences tend to be called feasts and are almost exclusively associated with summer. One friend told me of the "hot fat crab and cold beer" signs they see along the coast that time of year where she lives in Delaware. And a Marylander I spoke to had just recently been to a big feast at which about ninety people had gone through ten bushels of blue crab. "They're events here," he told me. No doubt!

These feasts are most always held outdoors, big mounds of freshly steamed crab piled high on picnic tables, with lots of sweet corn on the cob, maybe watermelon, and other summer treats alongside. Oh, and cold beer. Lots and lots of cold beer. By one account it seems that Natty Boh (National Bohemian beer, to outsiders) is something of an unofficial blue crab beer of summer.

Some may feast while others feed, but whatever coast or tradition is behind it—indulging in your fill of outstanding crab while it's at its best is definitely the name of the game.

THE ROSEMARY, LEMON, and garlic roasted with the crab here penetrate the sweet meat with delicious subtlety while filling the kitchen with their wonderful aroma. This preparation is particularly good with raw crab portions, which will absorb the flavors more than precooked crabmeat will. If using king or snow leg portions, you'll one to use one and one-half to two pounds.

ROSEMARY ROASTED CRAB

MAKES 2 TO 4 SERVINGS

1   Preheat the oven to 450 degrees F.

2   Lay the crab portions in a 9-by-13-inch baking dish and top with the rosemary sprigs and lemon slices. Add the oil, garlic, and pepper flakes, and season generously with salt and pepper. Toss with your hands to coat the crab pieces with the seasonings, then arrange them in an even layer with most of the rosemary and lemon underneath. If using raw crab, roast the crab until the flesh is just opaque through (use body portions to judge doneness; their flesh will be more visible), about 15 minutes, or roast the precooked crab until it is heated through, 7 to 10 minutes.

3   Transfer the crab pieces to a serving platter, surround them with the rosemary sprigs and lemon slices, and serve.

Crab: any in-shell crab, cleaned and portioned (blue crab simply cleaned)

2 Dungeness crab (about 2 pounds each), cleaned and portioned (see page 34), shells lightly cracked if precooked

6 to 8 long sprigs fresh rosemary

1 large lemon, thinly sliced

¼ cup mild olive oil

4 cloves garlic, chopped

¼ teaspoon dried red pepper flakes

Kosher salt and freshly ground black pepper

NOT ONLY DO we like our freshly cooked Dungeness crab steaming hot in the West, but we also relish sitting down to chilled crab as well. This recipe presumes you'll be cooking the crab yourself, but if you buy cooked Dungeness from the market, you're 90 percent to dinner. The crab just need to be cleaned (unless you asked them to do so at the market, in which case make that 95 percent). Cut up a couple lemons, dish up some sauce, tuck a napkin under your chin, and have something crisp and cold to drink within easy reach. To upgrade that scenario, this lemon mayonnaise does the trick.

COLD CRACKED CRAB WITH LEMON MAYONNAISE

MAKES 2 TO 4 SERVINGS

Crab: any in-shell cooked crabmeat

FOR THE LEMON MAYONNAISE:

1 small lemon

1 large egg yolk

¾ cup mild olive oil

Kosher salt and freshly ground white pepper

2 uncooked Dungeness crab (about 2 pounds each), live or cleaned and portioned (see page 34)

Lemon wedges, for serving

1 To make the lemon mayonnaise, finely grate ½ teaspoon of zest from the lemon and set it aside, then squeeze the juice from the lemon (you should have about 2 tablespoons).

2 In a medium bowl, combine 1 teaspoon of the lemon juice with the egg yolk and whisk to blend. Begin adding the oil, a couple drops at a time, whisking constantly, until the yolk begins to turn pale and thicken slightly, showing that an emulsion has begun to form. Continue adding the rest of the oil in a thin, steady stream, whisking constantly. Whisk in the remaining lemon juice with the lemon zest and salt and pepper to taste. Alternatively, combine the teaspoon of lemon juice and egg yolk in a food processor and pulse to blend. With the motor running, begin adding the oil a few drops at a time until an emulsion has begun to form, then continue adding the rest in a thin, steady stream. Add the remaining lemon juice

with the lemon zest and salt and pepper to taste, and pulse to blend.

3   Refrigerate the mayonnaise, covered, until ready to serve; it will have a fuller, more balanced flavor if made at least an hour before serving, and it can be made a day or two in advance.

4   Cook the crab as noted in Northwest Crab Boil (page 146). Carefully drain the crab and cool them completely in a large bowl (or sinkful) of ice water, then pat them dry. If you cooked whole crab, clean and portion them (see page 34). If not serving right away, you can refrigerate the crab for 1 to 2 hours.

5   Arrange the chilled crab portions on individual plates. Spoon the lemon mayonnaise into small dishes and serve it alongside the crab with the lemon wedges.

MAKING MAYO

Making mayonnaise by hand, with just a bowl and a whisk, is rewarding though it does take some dexterity to hold the bowl and drizzle the oil with one hand while whisking constantly with the other. One trick involves a kitchen towel: Grab the towel by opposite corners and twist them to make a long, slender roll, then wrap the roll around the base of the mixing bowl, gently tying it to secure a nest-like loop beneath the bowl. This will help keep the bowl from bouncing around too much as you work.

I've offered a quick food processor option as well—though it's important to note that if the blades of the processor aren't making contact with the little bit of liquid in the machine at the start, it can be difficult to get that initial emulsion going. Making mayonnaise by hand may take a bit more work, but you have more control over the mechanics of the process.

THE ORIGINS OF this recipe are a matter of effective sustenance rather that culinary splendor. It comes from the family of "catch of the day" seafood soups and stews that developed on fishing boats or docks around the globe, the crew using staple ingredients they had on hand with the addition of some of the day's catch. Often cioppino includes a range of seafoods such as clams, mussels, cubed fish, squid, and/or shrimp. I, however, think it really shines with nothing but crab, simmered in an herb- and vegetable-rich broth. Crusty bread—or better yet, garlic bread—is de rigueur alongside this redolent stew, as are plenty of napkins. Crab bibs too, if you have them. It's messy but worth it.

ALL-CRAB CIOPPINO

MAKES 4 TO 6 SERVINGS

Crab: cleaned Dungeness crab portions, snow or king crab legs

1 tablespoon mild olive oil

2 cups thinly sliced leeks, white and pale-green parts only

1 cup finely chopped onion

1 cup diced celery

2 tablespoons minced garlic

3 cups Crab Stock (page 111), fish stock, or chicken broth

1 (28-ounce) can top-quality diced tomatoes

1 Heat the oil in a large pot (about 8 quarts) over medium heat. Add the leeks, onion, celery, and garlic and cook until tender and aromatic, about 5 minutes, stirring occasionally. Add the stock, tomatoes, wine, tomato paste, lemon juice, bay leaves, basil, thyme, and pepper flakes with a good pinch each of salt and pepper. Bring just to a boil over medium-high heat, reduce the heat to low, and simmer, covered, for 15 minutes. Taste the broth for seasoning, adding more salt, pepper, or lemon juice to taste.

2 If any of the crab portions, particularly king or snow legs, are quite long, cut or break them in half crosswise for easier handling. On some legs there may be a joint near the center point, in which case you can simply bend the joint apart to separate the portions. Add the crab pieces to the pot, nestling them down into the liquids, and simmer, uncovered, until the crab is well heated, 10 to 12 minutes.

3   Use tongs to transfer the crab to individual large, shallow bowls, then ladle the rest of the stew over the crab. Tear the celery leaves into pieces and scatter them in the center of each bowl. Perch a lemon wedge to the side and serve.

½ cup dry red wine

¼ cup tomato paste

¼ cup freshly squeezed lemon juice (from about 1 large lemon or 2 small lemons), plus more to taste

2 bay leaves, preferably fresh

2 tablespoons finely chopped fresh basil

2 teaspoons finely chopped fresh thyme

¼ teaspoon dried red pepper flakes (optional)

Kosher salt and freshly ground black pepper

3 Dungeness crab (about 2 pounds each), cleaned and portioned (see page 34), shells lightly cracked if precooked

Handful tender celery leaves, for serving

Lemon wedges, for serving

YOU CAN TELL I'm not a native blue-crab eater, can't you? For one thing this recipe serves just a handful of folks, not a few dozen. I'm not cooking the blues by the bushel, or employing a backyard propane burner and ginormous pot. And the seasoning is subtle. This recipe is not intended to compete with the generations-old tradition of blue-crab feasts that stir up appetites in the East. This is a chance to bring some of that character inside. Cover the dinner table with newspaper to catch the scatterings of shell bits and crab while cracking through the meal. You'll be very happy come cleanup time when you can simply roll it all up for easy removal. Add corn on the cob and some cold beer— it'll be quite the minifeast.

Live blue crab don't travel all that well, though Asian markets and specialty seafood markets around the country will have them available beyond blue-crab country on occasion. Many of us must content ourselves with the long-distance second best: pre-cooked blue crab shipped to our doorstep.

BEER-STEAMED BLUE CRAB WITH MUSTARD BUTTER

MAKES 4 SERVINGS

1   Melt the butter in a small saucepan over medium heat. Take the pan from the heat, stir in the mustard powder, and set aside.

2   Pour the beer into a very large pot (see A Matter of Size on the following page), add the chiles, bay leaves, and parsley sprigs, and set a steamer basket in the bottom of the pot. Cover the pot and bring the beer to a boil over high heat. Add the crab, cover, reduce the heat to medium-high, and steam until the crab are

Crab: made with live or precooked blue crab in mind, but Dungeness crab portions or king or snow crab legs could be used

½ cup unsalted butter

1 teaspoon mustard powder

2 (12-ounce) bottles light- to medium-bodied beer

(CONTINUED)

5 to 6 dried red chiles, or
1 teaspoon dried red
pepper flakes

2 bay leaves, preferably
fresh, torn or crushed

6 to 8 sprigs fresh flat-leaf
(Italian) parsley

24 blue crab, live or
precooked

evenly bright red, 12 to 15 minutes if using live crab. (There should be plenty of liquid for this cooking time, but just to be safe check near the end and add a cup of boiling water if needed.) If using precooked crab, steam until heated through, about 5 minutes.

3 Use tongs to transfer the steamed crab to a large platter and set it in the center of the table. Stir the mustard butter to gently remix, then pour it into individual dishes for each guest to use. Have a bowl available for discarded shells, and provide plenty of napkins.

A MATTER OF SIZE

For this recipe, pull out the biggest pot you've got. A standard 8-quart stockpot will likely hold only about a dozen blue crab at a time, but the steaming is quick enough you can cook half at a time and serve the crab in two batches (if so, be sure there's enough liquid for the second batch; add more beer or water if needed). If you have one of those oversized seafood steamer pots that run in the 16-plus-quart range, it's a great time to use it.

THERE REALLY IS nothing better than pasta you've made yourself and cooked shortly after rolling and cutting the dough. Here the dough contains cilantro, adding a dash of color as well as a fresh herbal flavor to the noodles. Whole leaves are then tossed with the steaming noodles, crab, and lush butter for a simple but sophisticated finish. If you're a cilantrophobe, you can make this recipe with flat-leaf (Italian) parsley instead.

Since the butter here acts as a sauce of sorts, it's a rare time I'd recommend using salted butter if you have some, in which case little or no added salt may be needed when you're seasoning the finished dish. For a super shortcut or if you don't have a pasta machine, you could use top-quality dry fettuccine in place of the fresh pasta.

FRESH PASTA
WITH CRAB & CILANTRO

MAKES 2 TO 4 SERVINGS

1 Put the flour in a food processor with the salt and pulse once to blend. Add the eggs and pulse a few times to partially blend, then add the chopped cilantro and pulse until evenly blended. Transfer the dough to a work surface, form it into a ball, and knead it for a few minutes to create a cohesive, satiny dough, adding a bit more flour if the dough is still a little sticky. Wrap the dough in plastic and set it aside at room temperature for about 30 minutes.

2 Cut the pasta dough in half. Flatten one half with the heel of your hand into a rough rectangle that's a few inches wide and 4 to 5 inches long. Lightly dust the dough with flour, and roll it through the widest

Crab: any cooked crabmeat, mix of flake and lump ideal

1¼ cups all-purpose flour, plus more for rolling out pasta

½ teaspoon kosher salt

2 large eggs

2 tablespoons finely chopped fresh cilantro

8 ounces crabmeat

6 tablespoons salted butter, cut into 6 pieces

1 cup moderately packed fresh cilantro leaves

Kosher salt and freshly ground white pepper

¼ cup toasted pine nuts

(CONTINUED)

setting of a pasta machine. Fold the ends inward so that the dough is shaped like a packet about 4 inches across, flatten a bit with your hand again and run the pasta through the rollers, with the folded edges at either side and feeding one of the open edges in first. Repeat this process 4 or 5 more times to further knead the dough and make it very smooth, dusting the dough very lightly with flour as needed. Decrease the roller width by one setting and pass the full length of the pasta sheet through the rollers. Continue rolling out the dough at thinner and thinner settings until it is about $\frac{1}{16}$ inch thick.

3 Drape the pasta on a pasta rack or over the back of a chair that's been covered with a kitchen towel. Repeat the rolling process with the remaining dough. Let the dough sheets rest for about 30 minutes before continuing.

4 Scatter about ¼ cup of flour on a tray or rimmed baking sheet. Cut the first sheet of dough in half crosswise to make it easier to handle, and then pass each half through the wider fettuccine blades of the pasta cutter. Set the noodles in a nest on the floured tray, tossing gently to be sure they don't stick together. Repeat with the remaining dough.

5 Bring a large pot of generously salted water to a boil over high heat. While the water's heating, pick over the crabmeat to remove any bits of shell or cartilage. If using king or snow crab leg meat, cut it into medium dice.

6 When the water is at a full boil, add the pasta and boil just until al dente, about 1 minute. Drain the pasta well. Set the empty pot back over medium heat, and let it sit for a few moments until all the water has evaporated. Add the butter to the pot and stir until partly melted, then add the drained pasta and toss to coat it evenly with the butter. Add the cilantro leaves and crab, season with salt and pepper to taste, and toss to mix. Transfer the pasta to a large warmed bowl or individual plates, scatter the pine nuts over, and serve right away.

CRISP, SWEET SNAP peas make an ideal partner for sweet, tender crab in this quick stir-fry. The vibrant flavor of fresh ginger adds zip, both in the sauce and fried for garnishing the dish.

STIR-FRIED SNAP PEAS WITH CRAB & GINGER

MAKES 4 SERVINGS

1 Heat about ½ inch of oil in a small saucepan over medium-high heat. When hot (test with a piece of julienned ginger; the oil should bubble actively around it when added), add the julienned ginger and fry, stirring gently with a fork to keep the strands separated, until just lightly browned, about 1 minute. Use the fork to transfer the ginger to paper towels to drain; reserve the oil. In a small dish, combine the stock and cornstarch and stir to mix.

2 Pick over the crabmeat to remove any bits of shell or cartilage. If using king or snow crab leg meat, cut it into 1- to 2-inch pieces.

3 Scoop 2 tablespoons of the frying oil carefully from the saucepan into a wok or large, heavy skillet (discard the remaining oil or save for another use). Heat the oil over medium-high heat, then add the minced ginger and cook until aromatic, 10 to 15 seconds. Add the green onion; cook for about 1 minute longer. Add the peas and stir-fry until bright green and partly tender, about 2 minutes. Add the sake and simmer until reduced by about half, 1 to 2 minutes.

Crab: any cooked crabmeat

Mild olive or vegetable oil, for frying

2 tablespoons julienned peeled ginger

½ cup Crab Stock (page 111), fish stock, or chicken broth

2 teaspoons cornstarch

8 ounces crabmeat

2 tablespoons minced peeled ginger

¾ cup sliced green onion

12 ounces snap peas

½ cup sake or dry vermouth

1 tablespoon soy sauce, plus more to taste

3 to 4 cups steamed white or brown rice

(CONTINUED)

163

Main Courses

4 Stir the stock/cornstarch mixture to remix, then add it to the pan. Reduce the heat to medium low and cook until the sauce is thickened, about 2 minutes, stirring often. Add the crab and soy sauce to the peas and toss gently to warm through, 1 to 2 minutes. Taste for seasoning, adding more soy sauce to taste. Spoon the crab and peas over the rice on a serving platter or individual plates, scatter the fried ginger on top, and serve right away.

THIS IS ONE of my all-time favorite crab dishes, inspired by a dish I loved at the original Flying Fish restaurant located in Seattle's Belltown neighborhood. It will have you delightedly slurping crabmeat from its shells and licking your fingers. If you double the recipe—whether to serve four or offer a whole crab per serving—the original amount of spices will still suffice. Echoing its Asian roots, the crab is served with nam pla prik, a boldly flavored dipping sauce that's very quick to make.

SALT & PEPPER CRAB

MAKES 2 SERVINGS

1   To make the *nam pla prik*, in a small bowl, combine the fish sauce, lime juice, chiles, and garlic, stir to mix, and set aside. The sauce can be made a few hours in advance and refrigerated until ready to serve. Keep in mind that the longer the sauce sits, the more heat it will take on from the chiles.

2   In a small dish, combine the salt, black pepper, and Szechwan pepper and stir to mix. Heat the oil in a wok or large, heavy skillet over medium-high heat until just starting to smoke. Carefully add the crab pieces and stir-fry until heated, 3 to 4 minutes. Sprinkle the spice mixture over the crab and continue stir-frying until the pieces are evenly coated in the spices and they give off a slightly toasty aroma, about 2 minutes more.

3   Transfer the crab to a warmed serving platter. Pour the *nam pla prik* into individual bowls and serve alongside for dipping.

Crab: any in-shell cooked crab, cleaned and portioned

FOR THE *NAM PLA PRIK*:

¼ cup fish sauce

¼ cup freshly squeezed lime juice (from about 2 medium limes)

4 Thai green chiles, chopped

1 clove garlic, minced

1 teaspoon kosher salt

1 teaspoon freshly ground black pepper

1 teaspoon lightly crushed Szechwan pepper

2 tablespoons vegetable oil

1 cooked Dungeness crab (about 2 pounds), cleaned and portioned (see page 34), shells lightly cracked

THE SWEET AND tender crabmeat offers a distinct contrast to the nutty rice and earthy mushrooms in this risotto. The crop of wild chanterelles is often at its peak in the damp, mild fall and generally continues until the first frost. When chanterelles aren't available, you can use shiitake, cremini, or even everyday white button mushrooms in their place.

If using homemade crab stock, the roasted version will be particularly delicious here. And you might consider one additional step to finish this risotto with an extra dash of luxurious flavor: Put a couple cups of the crab stock in a saucepan and simmer over medium-high heat until reduced to about one-third cup. It will thicken slightly and become richer in color with concentrated flavor. Drizzle some of this over the risotto just before serving.

CRAB & CHANTERELLE RISOTTO

MAKES 4 SERVINGS

Crab: any cooked crabmeat, mix of flake and lump ideal

4 tablespoons unsalted butter, divided

8 ounces chanterelle mushrooms, wiped clean, trimmed, and sliced

1 cup dry white wine

3 cups Crab Stock (page 111) or chicken broth

½ cup finely chopped onion

1 cup arborio rice

8 to 12 ounces crabmeat

1   Melt 2 tablespoons of the butter in a medium skillet over medium-high heat. Add the mushrooms and sauté, stirring frequently, until they are tender and lightly browned, 4 to 5 minutes. Transfer the mushrooms to a bowl and set aside.

2   Add the wine to the skillet and bring to a boil, stirring to draw up any remaining cooking juices and flavors from the mushrooms. Pour the wine into a medium saucepan, add the crab stock, and bring just to a boil over medium-high heat. Immediately reduce the heat to low and keep warm.

3   Melt the remaining 2 tablespoons of the butter in a medium, heavy saucepan over medium heat. Add the onion and stir until tender and aromatic, about 3 minutes. The onion should soften but not brown. Add the rice and stir gently until it is evenly blended with the onion. Scoop about 1 cup of the warm stock into the rice and cook, stirring constantly, until the rice has absorbed most of the liquid, 3 to 5 minutes. Continue adding the stock, ½ cup at a time, stirring the rice constantly until most of the liquid is absorbed before adding the next, until the risotto is thick and creamy, and the rice is tender but not too soft—there should still be a bit of resistance at the center of each grain. You may not need every drop of the stock; total cooking time will be 30 to 40 minutes.

Kosher salt and freshly ground black pepper

2 tablespoons minced fresh flat-leaf (Italian) parsley

4 Pick over the crabmeat to remove any bits of shell or cartilage. If using king or snow crab leg meat, cut it into medium dice. Add the crab and mushrooms to the risotto with a good pinch of salt and a pinch of pepper (more salt will be needed if using crab stock than chicken broth). Let heat for a few minutes, stirring occasionally, until warmed through. Spoon the risotto into warmed shallow bowls and sprinkle the parsley over it.

THIS ECHOES HALF of the elaborate king crab feast that's a signature experience at Sun Sui Wah Seafood Restaurant in Vancouver, British Columbia. When available, live king crab will be lounging in the restaurant's huge tanks, plucked to order, and presented in all its thorny glory to your table before being whisked into the kitchen for cooking. The crab's generally cooked two ways: the body meat portioned and stir-fried with chile peppers and coarse salt, and the legs steamed with a garlicky topping. This is my interpretation of the latter service, just a few ingredients needed to flavor the rich crab. You'll likely find king crab portions frozen, in which case budget time for thawing (see page 28 for thawing notes).

STEAMED KING CRAB WITH GARLIC

MAKES 2 TO 4 SERVINGS

Crab: in-shell portions of king or snow crab

2 teaspoons mild olive oil or vegetable oil

¼ cup chopped garlic (8 to 10 cloves)

8 tablespoons thinly sliced green onion, divided

1 tablespoon toasted sesame oil

2 teaspoons Shaoxing wine (Chinese rice wine), dry sherry, or dry white wine

¼ teaspoon kosher salt

2 pounds thawed king or snow crab leg portions

1 Heat the olive oil in a small skillet over medium-low heat. Add the garlic and 4 tablespoons of the green onion and cook gently, stirring occasionally, until the garlic is tender but not browned, 3 to 5 minutes. Transfer the mixture to a small bowl and stir in the sesame oil, wine, and salt.

2 Use a cleaver or other large, heavy knife to cut the longer crab legs in half crosswise for easier handling. On some legs there may be a joint near the center point, in which case you can instead simply bend the joint apart to separate the portions. Then use slender-bladed kitchen shears to cut a slit ¼ to ½ inch wide the length of one side of each crab portion, exposing the meat slightly so flavors infuse into it

more and making it easier to extract the meat later. To decide where on the leg to make this slit, set the crab piece on the counter and see which side sits flat most naturally; cut the shell on the top side in this position.

3   Put a few inches of water in a wok or large pot over which a double-layer bamboo steamer basket will fit snugly. Bring the water to a boil over high heat.

4   While the water is heating, set a heatproof plate inside each of the steamer baskets and lay the crab pieces on the plates. Spoon the garlic mixture over the crab pieces, aiming to land across the split opening as much as possible. Stack the baskets over the boiling water, cover, and steam until the crab is heated through, 8 to 10 minutes. Transfer the crab leg portions to a platter or individual plates, scatter the remaining 4 tablespoons green onion over, and serve right away.

IF YOU HAVEN'T thought about grilling crab before, you're going to be happy to add this to your repertoire. It offers the traditional benefit of outdoor character that comes into play anytime you grill, with an added dose of flavor from the toasty crab shells imparting a slightly nutty flavor. In this recipe that flavor gets embellished with orange that both coats the shells before grilling and becomes part of the buttery sauce used for dipping. And the sauce has a dash of rum as well!

GRILLED CRAB WITH CHARRED ORANGE-RUM BUTTER

MAKES 4 TO 6 SERVINGS

Crab: Dungeness crab sections, king or snow crab legs, cleaned whole blue crab

2 Dungeness crab (about 2 pounds each), cleaned and portioned (see page 34), shells lightly cracked if precooked

1 large navel orange

¼ cup mild olive oil

Kosher salt and freshly ground black pepper

½ cup unsalted butter

3 tablespoons rum

3 dashes Angostura bitters (optional)

1   If any of the crab portions, particularly king or snow legs, are quite long, cut or break them in half crosswise for easier handling. On some legs there may be a joint near the center point, in which case you can simply bend the joint apart to separate the portions. Put the crab portions in a large bowl or large roasting pan (you need enough room to be able to toss the crab with seasonings).

2   Grate the zest from the orange and set aside ½ teaspoon for the butter sauce. Put the remaining zest in a small bowl and stir in the oil with a good pinch each of salt and pepper. Pour this over the crab pieces and toss to coat them as evenly as you're able. Set aside.

3   Preheat an outdoor grill to medium-high heat.

4 In a small saucepan, combine the butter, rum, bitters, and reserved orange zest. Add a good pinch of salt and warm over medium-low heat until the butter is melted. Set aside.

5 Cut the orange into eighths. When the grill is hot, grill the orange pieces until the flesh is lightly charred, 2 to 3 minutes on each of the wedges. Set the charred orange wedges aside.

6 Arrange the crab pieces on the grill and cook, turning every couple of minutes, until lightly browned and aromatic, about 6 to 8 minutes total. By this time precooked crab should be fully warmed; if you started with raw crab continue cooking for 5 to 7 minutes more, until the exposed body meat is cooked through and no longer translucent.

7 Arrange the grilled crab on a platter with 6 of the orange wedges around the crab. Squeeze the remaining 2 orange wedges into the butter sauce and stir to blend. Pour the butter into individual small bowls and set them on plates, passing the crab for guests to serve themselves.

ACKNOWLEDGMENTS

Among the many crab specialists with whom I spoke, Rich Childers and
Dan Ayres from the Washington Department of Fish and Wildlife; Hugh
Link, executive director of the Oregon Dungeness Crab Commission;
Bill Brooks at J. M. Clayton Company in Maryland; Glenn Davis with the
Maryland Department of Natural Resources; Jennifer Shriver from the
Alaska Department of Fish and Game; and Dan Ellinor with Florida Fish
and Wildlife Conservation Commission were all exceptionally helpful
with nitty-gritty details about crab.

It was a treat to reconnect with a colleague dating back to my time
at *Simply Seafood* magazine. John van Amerongen, now at Trident
Seafoods, helped me cover a lot of interesting (and delicious) territory
related to king and snow crab. Thanks to Harry and Kevin Yoshimura
and the whole crew at Mutual Fish in Seattle. Cheers also to Karl Uri at
Alaska Seafood Marketing Institute for assisting with crab corralling.

Tom and Melissa Willits from Kathi's Krabs in Florida made me a very happy cookbook author by sending some gorgeous first-of-the-season stone crab claws just in time for this book deadline!

Among those who shared with me a lot of their own passion for crab include Riki Senn (my Delaware blue-crab correspondent), and fellow Dungeness enthusiasts Stephanie and Andy Hogenson, Victoria Trimmer, and Serni Solidarios.

It was a great pleasure to work again with photographer Jim Henkens. I adore his talent for capturing the essence of his subject. And many thanks to Gary, Em, Joyce, Rebekah, and the rest of the Sasquatch team!

I was fortunate to have a few great palates helping me navigate the beverage options for crab, which include Dawn Smith, Bryan Maletis, and Jameson Fink. And I'm always so thankful to dear friends who are willing and enthusiastic recipe tasters, offering great feedback and sometimes just the perfect tweak to make the recipe even better.

INDEX

NOTE: *Photographs are indicated by italics.*

CONVERSIONS

VOLUME

UNITED STATES	METRIC	IMPERIAL
¼ tsp.	1.25 ml	
½ tsp.	2.5 ml	
1 tsp.	5 ml	
½ Tbsp.	7.5 ml	
1 Tbsp.	15 ml	
⅛ c.	30 ml	1 fl. oz.
¼ c.	60 ml	2 fl. oz.
⅓ c.	80 ml	2.5 fl. oz.
½ c.	125 ml	4 fl. oz.
1 c.	250 ml	8 fl. oz.
2 c. (1 pt.)	500 ml	16 fl. oz.
1 qt.	1 l	32 fl. oz.

LENGTH

UNITED STATES	METRIC
⅛ in.	3 mm
¼ in.	6 mm
½ in.	1.25 cm
1 in.	2.5 cm
1 ft.	30 cm

WEIGHT

AVOIRDUPOIS	METRIC
¼ oz.	7 g
½ oz.	15 g
1 oz.	30 g
2 oz.	60 g
3 oz.	90 g
4 oz.	115 g
5 oz.	150 g
6 oz.	175 g
7 oz.	200 g
8 oz. (½ lb.)	225 g
9 oz.	250 g
10 oz.	300 g
11 oz.	325 g
12 oz.	350 g
13 oz.	375 g
14 oz.	400 g
15 oz.	425 g
16 oz. (1 lb.)	450 g
1½ lb.	750 g
2 lb.	900 g
2¼ lb.	1 kg
3 lb.	1.4 kg
4 lb.	1.8 kg

TEMPERATURE

OVEN MARK	FAHRENHEIT	CELSIUS	GAS
Very cool	250–275	130–140	½–1
Cool	300	150	2
Warm	325	165	3
Moderate	350	175	4
Moderately hot	375	190	5
	400	200	6
Hot	425	220	7
	450	230	8
Very Hot	475	245	9

ABOUT THE AUTHOR

CYNTHIA NIMS is a lifelong Northwesterner who reveled in growing up surrounded by great food—both in her mother's kitchen and exploring the region with her family, whether eating grilled oysters on a San Juan Island beach or huckleberry pancakes while backpacking in the Olympic Mountains. After graduating from the University of Puget Sound, having majored in mathematics and French literature, Cynthia followed her dreams and went to France to study cooking at La Varenne Ecole de Cuisine. There, she received the Grand Diplôme d'Etudes Culinaires and worked on numerous cookbooks with the school's president, Anne Willan, including *Great Cooks and Their Recipes* and ten in the Look & Cook series.

Cynthia is the author of over a dozen cookbooks, which includes *Oysters*, released in early 2016. Her latest cookbooks were produced on Kindle, including *Crab*, *Wild Mushrooms*, *Salmon*, and four other titles in the Northwest Cookbooks series. She was also among the team of writers and editors for the groundbreaking Modernist Cuisine volumes released in 2011 and served as a writer for *The Photography of Modernist Cuisine* released in 2013.

Previously the editor of *Simply Seafood* magazine and food editor of *Seattle Magazine*, she has since been a contributor to *Cooking Light*, *Coastal Living*, *Alaska Airlines Magazine*, *Sunset*, and other magazines. She is an active member of the International Association of Culinary Professionals (having served as president of the board) and Les Dames d'Escoffier. Her blog, *Mon Appétit*, can be found at MonAppetit.com. Cynthia and her husband live in Seattle, WA.